Better Homes and Gardens®

celebrate the
SEASON®

contents

fall

trims

food

gifts

120 SHARE YOUR TALENTS with those on your holiday gift list. Everyone feels more special receiving gifts that come from the heart. Cleverly packaged foods, initial coasters, and more inspire your creative side. And when it comes to presenting these treasures, count on joyful gift wrap ideas.

kids

140 ENCOURAGE LITTLE ONES to create gifts and decorations this holiday season. With a little guidance from you, kids of all ages can make awesome projects to encourage their love of crafting. Just wait until you see their faces light up when they present a loved one with a gift they made by hand— priceless!

in a twinkling

CLEVER AND QUICK, these projects can be accomplished at the last minute—and no one has to know!

MEREDITH CONSUMER MARKETING
Consumer Marketing Product Director: Heather Sorensen
Consumer Marketing Product Manager: Wendy Merical
Consumer Marketing Billing/Renewal Manager: Tami Beachem
Business Director: Ron Clingman
Senior Production Manager: Al Rodruck

WATERBURY PUBLICATIONS, INC.
Contributing Editor: Sue Banker
Contributing Art Director: Cathy Brett
Contributing Food Stylists: Jennifer Peterson, Charles Worthington
Contributing Copy Editor: Terri Fredrickson
Contributing Proofreader: Peg Smith
Editorial Director: Lisa Kingsley
Creative Director: Ken Carlson
Associate Editors: Tricia Bergman, Mary Williams
Associate Design Director: Doug Samuelson
Production Assistant: Mindy Samuelson

BETTER HOMES AND GARDENS₈ MAGAZINE
Editor in Chief: Gayle Goodson Butler
Executive Editor: Oma Blaise Ford
Managing Editor: Gregory H. Kayko
Creative Director: Michael D. Belknap
Senior Deputy Editor, Food and Entertaining: Nancy Wall Hopkins

MEREDITH NATIONAL MEDIA GROUP
President: Tom Harty

MEREDITH CORPORATION
Chairman and Chief Executive Officer: Stephen M. Lacy

In Memoriam: E.T. Meredith III (1933–2003)

you're the one

Get ready to make the holidays special for everyone you love. *Better Homes and Gardens® Celebrate the Season* makes it easy for you to become a party planner, decorator, and chef extraordinaire.

Your creative portfolio will burst at the seams, armed with fresh crafts ideas to transform your home into a festive wonderland. You'll discover table settings, wreaths, party favors, ornaments—mounds of merry ideas to feed your creative side.

And your recipe box is about to expand too! Appetizers, main courses, sides, desserts—delicious sensations guaranteed to leave family and friends raving about your cooking talents. Many of the recipes are sure make your go-to-favorites list to enjoy year round.

And the kids? *Celebrate the Season* offers fun crafts for them too. They can hop on the creative wagon by making ornaments, favors, decorations, and more—adorable projects to display with pride.

So here's to you—crafts queen, kitchen conqueror, decorating diva, and creative coach. Enjoy your new titles as you bask in the glow of the holidays. After all, you're the one who is about to become the memory-maker of all time.

With sincere wishes for the best holiday season ever,

Sue Banker

fall

THE COLORFUL CALM

TAKE IT ALL IN

Enjoy this time of thanks—welcoming it in with projects that honor the blissful autumn season.

Tray Chic

Flea-market trays get a fresh look with paint and pattern.

Delightfully Edgy

Tout a natural look with jute and rich, soft art paper. To line both sides of a metal tray, brush on a thick coat of decoupage medium then gently press the paper onto the glue. Smooth out wrinkles as much as possible; trim around edge and let glue dry. Hot-glue jute rope along the edge of tray. Brush top of rope with metallic paint and let dry.

Lacy Shadows

Two colors of spray paint and a few paper doilies are all it takes to achieve this lacy look. Spray the tray with the base paint color and let dry. Place a few doilies over the tray and spray lightly with second color; remove doilies and let dry. To add depth to the finish, place more doilies on larger solid areas of the tray and spray with the base color. Want to turn the tray into a pedestal server? Glue a wide candleholder to the bottom. When dry, invert the tray and spray-paint the bottom to match.

Pattern Play

Tone-on-tone color is the key to this interesting tray inset. Choose laser-cut wood pieces, readily available at crafts stores, to fit inside a metal tray. Using the photo on page 10 as a guide, arrange the wood pieces in the tray as desired. Work one piece at a time and adhere the pieces in place using strong adhesive, such as CA glue. When the glue is completely set, spray the tray with several light coats of paint, drying between coats. Be sure to work in a well-ventilated area.

All Cracked Up

Conceal a marred and tarnished surface with a welcome coat of crackle that carries out a timeworn piece in stylish fashion. While this tray was painted gold with burnt umber enhancing the cracks, you can choose any color combination to blend with your decor. Follow the instructions on the crackling medium to achieve the desired look. Most crackle mediums have a base coat, crackle, and enhancer. For an upscale look, add a handle to each end of the tray. Drill holes warranted by the handle and attach with short bolts.

Lovely Lining

Line a rectangular tray with a soft layer of three coordinating fabrics. Measure the tray inset and divide the length into thirds. Cut three coordinating pieces of fabric to size. Adhere the fabric pieces to the tray using decoupage medium; let dry. To finish the edges, use strong double-stick tape to adhere grosgrain ribbons between fabric pieces, then around edges, with ends wrapping around sides of tray.

Gourds of Beauty

Works-of-art gourds offer one more thing from the autumn season for which to be thankful.

GORGEOUS GINKO
instructions on page 14

NATURAL WINNERS
instructions on page 14

Gorgeous Ginko
Pictured on page 12
Transform a canteen gourd into an intricate lidded masterpiece.

WHAT YOU NEED for the ginko gourd
Flexible tape measure; pencil
Dried canteen gourd
Large and small ginko leaf
Thin plastic, such as a food container lid
Micro-saw or other cutting tool, such as a Versa Tool that also woodburns
Dust mask
Metal spoon
Fine-grit sandpaper
Spray clear sealer; paint (optional)
Light shade of leather dye

WHAT YOU DO
1. Use tape measure to mark eight equal vertical spaces around gourd.
2. Draw or trace around one large and one small ginko leaf onto a thin piece of plastic for a stencil. Using the lines as placement guides, trace around stencil onto gourd, overlapping leaves in a pleasing arrangement.
3. Woodburn along pencil lines, adding veins on leaves. Using a cutting tool, cut through the gourd along the bottom edge of the leaves. Remove lid, clean, and seal or paint inside of the gourd as for "Natural Winners", below.
4. Use a light color of leather dye to color leaves and a darker tone for background. When dry, spray with a clear finish in a well-ventilated work area. Let dry.

Natural Winners
Pictured on page 13
Green inks enhance artistic accents.

WHAT YOU NEED for the wave gourd
Pencil with eraser
Dried cannonball gourd
Dust mask
Micro-saw or other cutting tool, such as a Versa Tool that also woodburns
Metal spoon
Fine-grit sandpaper
Black spray paint
Drill with 1/32-inch bit
Woodburning tool
Flexible tape measure

Alcohol ink in desired color(s), usually found near stamping ink pads in crafts stores
Cotton swab, small cotton pad, paintbrush, or mister
Heat gun or hair dryer
Spray clear sealer
Sewing needle
Artificial sinew or other fiber
Green Danish cord or other cording

WHAT YOU DO
1. With a pencil, draw a circle around top of gourd. Wearing a dust mask, cut off gourd top with a micro-saw or other cutting tool. Scrape out inside with a spoon and sand smoothly inside and outside. In a well-ventilated work area, finish inside with black spray paint, being careful not to get paint on the outside of the gourd. Let it dry.
2. Draw a line around gourd top approximately ¾ inch from rim. Using photo as a guide, draw a wavy design to allow for three openings. Woodburn a line approximately 1 inch below wavy line. Cut out open spaces. Erase extra markings.
3. Measure and drill holes every ½ inch for coiling around the rim and in the wavy section halfway between the woodburned line and the cut-out area.
4. Use alcohol ink to color bottom part of gourd. Apply ink with a cotton swab, small cotton pad, paintbrush, or mister. The effect may look dappled. Practice on a cut-off piece of gourd to achieve the desired look. Follow the alcohol ink instructions for heat setting, then spray on a clear finish and let dry.
5. Thread sinew through a sewing needle. Starting with the wavy section, use sinew to stitch two rows of cord to gourd. Repeat with gourd rim. After the first round is attached, add six more rounds, stitching cording to previous round.

WHAT YOU NEED for the leaf silhouette gourd
Pencil with eraser
Dried kettle gourd
Dust mask
Micro-saw or other cutting tool, such as a Versa Tool that also woodburns

Metal spoon
Fine-grit sandpaper
Black spray paint
Drill with 1/32-inch bit
Adhesive vinyl with backing
Sharp crafts knife
Woodburning tool
Flexible tape measure
Alcohol ink in desired color(s), usually found near stamping ink pads in crafts stores
Small cotton pad
Heat gun or hair dryer
Paste wax
Sewing needle
Artificial sinew or other fiber
Green Danish cord or other cording

WHAT YOU DO
1. With a pencil, draw an angled circle around the top of gourd. Wearing a dust mask, cut off the gourd top with a micro-saw or other cutting tool. Scrape out the inside with a spoon and sand smoothly inside and outside. In a well-ventilated work area, spray the inside with black paint. Let it dry.
2. Measure and drill holes every ½ inch for coiling around the rim.
3. On vinyl, draw willow leaves of various sizes and narrow strips for stems. Use a sharp crafts knife to cut through vinyl around pattern, but not through backing.
4. Apply the stems and leaves on the gourd, leaving space between them.
5. Use a light color alcohol ink on a cotton pad and dab it so some areas are more saturated. Cover most of surface with color and use heat gun to set color. Repeat these steps with a medium color and a third time with a bit darker color, heat-setting each layer.
6. After the third layer is dry, peel off all vinyl leaves, revealing the resist pattern. Again, heat the gourd and use several layers of paste wax to seal and shine the gourd, polishing between coats with a soft cloth.
7. Thread sinew through a sewing needle. Use sinew to sew cord around the rim.

Oak-Go-Round

Handsome oak leaves are the main attraction on this kettle gourd.

WHAT YOU NEED for the oak leaf gourd

Flexible tape measure; pencil
Dried kettle gourd
Oak leaf
Thin plastic, such as a food container lid
Oval cutter
Micro-saw or other cutting tool, such as a Versa Tool that also woodburns
Dust mask
Metal spoon
Fine-grit sandpaper
Spray clear sealer; paint (optional)
White masking fluid, found near watercolor paints in crafts stores
Alcohol ink in desired color(s), usually found near stamping ink pads in crafts stores
Small spritzer bottle
Heat gun
Clear finishing spray or paste wax

WHAT YOU DO

1. Use a flexible tape measure to mark six equal vertical spaces around gourd.
2. Draw or trace around an oak leaf onto a thin piece of plastic for a stencil.
3. Using the lines as placement guides, center stencil in each section, then trace around stencil onto gourd. Use an oval cutter to make a frame just larger than leaf; cut out and trace around each leaf.
4. Woodburn along pencil lines. Using a cutting tool, cut through gourd along top edge of ovals to make a lid.
5. Remove lid, clean, and seal or paint inside of gourd as for Natural Winners.
6. Use white masking fluid to cover areas that you want to remain natural; let dry.
7. Put alcohol inks in small spritzer bottles and lightly apply several colors. Let the colors blend together naturally, creating a modeled effect.
8. Peel off masking fluid and set the color with a heat gun.
9. Finish with a clear finishing spray or paste wax.

Be Thankful

Celebrate Thanksgiving with lovingly crafted tabletop trimmings to make holiday guests feel extra special.

Initial Reaction

For a new take on a place card, monogram precut paper discs with rub-on transfer letters. Tuck under a glass salad plate.

Ring Around

Give napkin rings a new fall wardrobe. Wrap with strips of paper or ribbon, secure with double-sided tape, and hot-glue buttons or metal charms from a crafts store. This easy trick works on any napkin ring with a smooth exterior surface.

Let There Be Light

Pop votive candles into ordinary glass tumblers— safer at the table than an open flame—and surround the votive candleholders with unshelled nuts. Transparent glass with wide openings work best.

Market Masterpiece

Pick up everything you need for a stunning centerpiece while shopping for groceries. Choose fruit and flowers in the same hue. Arrange the fruit in the bottom of a compote, add an inch of water, then tuck in flowers, greenery, and nuts.

Turn Over a New Leaf

Bring a touch of nature to the table by gracing each plate with a silk leaf pressed under a clear glass plate. For added pizzazz, outline each leaf and enhance the veins using metallic gold thread and running stitches.

Foiled Again

Foil-wrapped candies seem to pop up during every holiday, and turkeys are a favorite for Thanksgiving. Choose those that stand up, and place one on each guest's plate. To mimic the foil look, wad tin foil then gently flatten it. Form it around a plate charger, taping edges to the underside. Choose a color or two from the candy foil and match to metallic acrylic paint. Use a foam brush to lightly paint the charger, wiping raised areas with a paper towel to allow the silver foil to shine through.

Shimmer and Shine

If metallic is the showstopper at your Thanksgiving table, these pumpkins will blend right in. To give artificial pumpkins a metallic coat, wad tin foil then gently flatten it. Form it around the pumpkin, poking a hole in the center for the stem. Trim away excess foil and hot-glue edges to the bottom. Use a foam brush to paint raised areas and stem with copper paint; let dry.

Pretty Pick

Be thankful for a long guest list while keeping the dinner table budget in check. Layer plastic dinner plates with Thanksgiving-theme dessert-size paper plates. For added wow, tie a ribbon bow onto a wired berry sprig and shape it to frame the corner of the plate.

Felt-Leaf Artwork

Jazz up your wall for fall with this easy autumn artwork. Simply mount felt leaf shapes, from a crafts store or cut your own, in shadow boxes with patterned-paper mats. Use decorative stickpins and colorful snips of ribbon to add even more festive flair.

Duplicating Nature

Using leaves as patterns, these fall decorations are as pretty as the season itself.

Leafy Window Banner

Use tissue paper and twigs to make a playful garland. Trace leaf shapes onto heavy cardstock to make templates. Cut them out and trace the shapes onto patterned tissue paper then cut out the leaves. Glue tiny twigs onto the leaves to create veining, then adhere the finished leaves on a narrow strip of twine. Hang the garland in a window.

Nice and Easy Pillow

Perk up a plain pillow. Enlarge a leaf using a copier to make a pattern. Cut the pattern out of wool felt and attach it to the pillow cover using iron-on fusible backing. Blanket-stitch around the edges.

Fallen Leaves Table Runner

You may have trouble keeping the piles of foliage outside in order, but these leaves march in perfect rows across a table runner. To make it, use a stencil or rubber stamp and fabric or crafts paint to decorate a plain linen cloth. Keep the job easy and the rows evenly spaced by cutting nine leaf designs into one 8½×11-inch piece of stencil paper. Follow instructions on the paint container for setting and washing the finished design.

Leaf Plates

Clearly stated, this tablescape uses fallen leaves as patterns to shine through clear glass plates. Trace around shapes on felt, burlap, linen, or other fabric then cut out. Place leaf shapes under plates to bring autumn's beauty to the table.

Seasonally Stamped Pillowcases

Count acorns and leaves rather than sheep as you drift off on pillowcases dressed for the season. To make a pillowcase, buy an inexpensive cotton case. Place cardboard between the layers. Stencil on the motifs using fabric paint. Follow the instructions on the paint container for setting and washing the finished design.

Natural Welcome
Bring a little slice of nature to your front door with a woodland-inspired wreath. Use either precut wood slices found at crafts stores or cut a branch into segments. Glue the pieces to a wooden wreath form and adorn with burlap ribbon, pinecones, greenery, and berries.

Lasting Beauty
Welcome fall with wreaths that transition right into Christmas. Natural hues make them perfect for both joyous seasons.

Fall Wheat Sheaves Wreath

Impress guests at first knock. Gather a bunch of dried wheat and secure together in the center using a rubber band. Use scissors to trim ends to the same length and finish with a wide silk or velvet ribbon.

Harvest Moon

A horseshoe shape is a welcome change for a traditional wreath. Start with a foam wreath form then cut away about one-fifth of the ring. Wrap with seam binding ribbon to cover foam. Using hot glue, attach fresh or preserved salal leaves (lemon leaves) as shown, along with a cluster of nuts in the center. Add dried wheat, preserved fern fronds, and fresh or silk berries.

Welcome Wheat Wreath

Spice up a traditional harvest wreath with metallic spray paint and a friendly welcome sign. To make, divide one bunch of dried wheat into three groups. Use a light touch to paint each group a different metallic finish, such as gold, copper, and brass. Wrap a foam wreath form with twine. Tuck unpainted stalks into the twine, randomly tucking in the painted wheat stems. Change the message when Christmas draws near.

In-A-Twinkling
Burlap Bliss

Beribboned Favors

Short cans, cardboard containers, or jars work perfectly for candy cup bases. Simply wrap a container with a strip of burlap or burlap ribbon and secure with a hefty plaid ribbon bow.

Layered Rings

Dress up a plain wooden napkin ring with a strip of burlap topped with decorative ribbon. Use hot glue to secure the burlap piece to the ring, then the ribbon to the burlap.

Thanksgiving Crackers

Encase traditional Christmastime "crackers" with messages of thanks along with seasonal sweets. To make one, wrap a short paper tube with art paper, leaving 3 inches on each end; tape in center. Tie one end with raffia and fill with a personalized message of Thanksgiving and wrapped candies. Tie the remaining end with raffia. Cut a piece of burlap to wrap tube; hot-glue in place. Trim tube with ribbon and a dimensional scrapbook embellishment.

Wheat Wrap

This autumnal accent will last for years to come. To make the everlasting bouquet, cut an oval from 3-inch-thick plastic foam. Trim wheat, leaving 5-inch-long stems, and gently poke them into foam to make a dense arrangement. Wrap foam with a 4-inch-wide piece of burlap, overlap ends, and secure with hot glue. Thread two fibers from burlap through holes in two large decorative buttons; knot each on the front and trim. Hot-glue buttons to front as shown.

Woven Beauty

Make a handsome place mat using a pulled-thread technique. Choose three ribbons without wired edges. Leave 1 inch intact at edge and pull burlap threads one at a time to allow for a ribbon. Wrap ribbon end with tape; cut into a point. Weave ribbon through pulled threads. Work in the remaining ribbons in same manner.

Cross-Stitch Coaster

Cushion cups with easy-to-stitch coasters. Cut two 5-inch squares from burlap; set one aside. Working over two threads with embroidery floss, cross-stitch as shown. Using pulled burlap fiber, stitch the layers together using running stitches.

trims

ALL AGLOW

As the tree goes up and you transform your home into a joyful wonderland, make it the most festive year ever with unforgettable decorations that brighten the season.

Wooden Wonders

Kick off winter with woodburned accents that offer cozy cabin warmth.

Under Wraps

Achieve a casual look with candles shining softly through canning jars. To dress up the jar, wrap with a wide band of plaid ribbon held in place with a trio of jute strings tied into a bow. Hot-glue a pinecone and sprig of artificial greenery just above the bow. For the finishing touch, woodburn snowflakes or dot designs into four wood beads, thread on four strings, then knot all ends.

Strung Along

Craft a woodsy garland to hang on the tree or to loop across the mantel or along a railing. Wood bead spacers aid in making the garland work up quickly. For accents, twist mini screw eyes into pinecone tops (poking first with an awl if needed) and drill holes through the center of branch slices. Thread onto string in a repetitive pattern.

Wintry Welcome

Freestyled or sketched out first in pencil, this fun plaque salutes the season. Referring to the photo, use a round tip to woodburn "Let it" in a series of dots and a straight tip for "SNOW." Burn snowflakes, trios of dots, and a dotted border to complete the sign.

Bowl of Plenty

For an interesting grouping, pile wood-burned pods and branch slices atop snippets of evergreen. Use extra caution burning pods as some are very thin skinned and dry. Use a cooler setting, if possible, or a light touch with the woodburning tool.

Everlasting Snowflakes

Wood coasters, still encased with bark, make great bases for woodburned snowflake ornaments. You can freestyle a snowflake or use these easy steps. After marking the center of the coaster with a pencil mark, use a ruler to draw a plus sign (+) and an X. Trace the lines with a woodburning tool as shown in Photo A. To make short lines, use a straight tip and press into wood as shown in Photo B. Use the same tip to score the edge as shown in Photo C. To make dots, use a round tip as shown in Photo D. Twist a screw eye into the top of the ornament, tie with a ribbon bow, and hang from thread.

Peppermint Party

Candy canes and peppermint disks, in traditional holiday hues, are natural ingredients for Christmas decorations.

Sweet Ride

Special delivery at your service. To make the sleigh, trace patterns on pages 154–155. Use patterns to cut pieces from mat board. With packing tape attach sides, front, and back to bottom of sleigh. Fold up back, sides, and front; tape at corners. Using photo as a guide, hot-glue peppermint disks to side panels, allowing candies to extend slightly beyond edges. Glue cinnamon drops between disks. Use scissors to cut small candy canes to cover the back and front panels. Glue on large candy cane runners. Finish side and back edges with decorative trim.

Ring Around the Candy

Sticks of small candy canes make a festive candy holder. Use scissors to cut pieces slightly shorter than a straight votive candleholder. With cut ends down, hot-glue candy cane pieces to candleholder then tie with ribbon.

Merry Go-Rounds

Perched on packages or hanging on the tree, candy wreaths can be made in minutes. Cut a 3-inch-diameter ring from cardboard. Hot-glue peppermint disks, cinnamon-drop berries, and a ribbon bow on the ring.

On the Edge

Pull off clever lighting when company is on the way. Hang small candy canes over the edge of votive candleholders and place a dinnerlight candle in the center.

Peppermint Snowflakes

Delightfully dainty, and perfect for catching winter's sun, candy-laden snowflakes can be fashioned in myriad patterns. To replicate this one, first make 11 heart shapes from regular-size candy canes. Hot-glue where candy canes touch. Glue a peppermint disk to each top point as shown in Photo A. Arrange the hearts in a circle as shown in Photo B and hot-glue where candy meets. Adhere more peppermint disks around center, as shown in Photo C. Gently turn over the snowflake. Cut candy cane pieces to fit heart tops as shown in Photo D; hot-glue in place. Turn snowflake back over. Use scissors to cut off rounded hook of 10 candy canes; hot-glue just above center disks as shown in Photo E. Glue the cut-off straight pieces just above the hooks as shown in photo, left. Paint a flat wood wreath form white; let dry. Hot-glue wreath form to back of candy cane wreath for support.

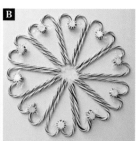

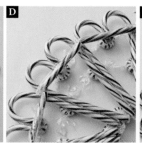

Candy Trees

Planted on a circle cut from foam core board, these peppermint trees share a touch of holiday whimsy. Use the patterns on page 155 to cut shapes from foam core board using a crafts knife. Glue green and white peppermint disks to the triangle as shown. Glue seven to nine red and white peppermint disks one atop the other to make a trunk; glue treetop to top of trunk. Glue bottom of trunk to foam core circle.

Attention Getter

Place a pretty section from a sweater over a cardboard star form (available from crafts stores) and cut, leaving 1 inch excess all around. Starting at the center and working outward, hot-glue to secure. Glue edges under the form.

Sweater Set

Old sweaters get a new spin as holiday decor. Grab your glue gun and deck the halls with these warm fuzzies leading the way.

Tabletop Trees

Sweater trees look cozy on a mantel or a dining table. Drill a hole for a ¼-inch-thick wooden dowel in a slice of wood. Dab hot glue in the hole and insert dowel; let dry. With a sweater inside out, cut two matching triangles, leaving ¼-inch seam allowance. Pin sides and sew, leaving a small gap in the center of the base. Turn right side out, stuff with polyfill, and insert the top of the dowel into the triangle. Glue closed to finish.

Wee Warmth

Spruce up your tree with miniature winter sweaters. Cut a mini torso shape and sleeve pieces that are 1 inch longer than you want the finished size. Round the top corners of the torso and pin sleeves in place, overlapping in back. Adhere heavy fusible interfacing to the back, according to manufacturer's instructions. Remove pins, and trim as needed. Cut a collar from sweater ribbing and attach with hot glue. Use a needle and thread to add a loop for hanging. For more ornaments, try hat, stocking, star, and mitten shapes.

Gifted Tags

Let Nordic motifs inspire your gift tags. Simply photocopy sections from knitwear, cut into a tag shape, punch a hole in the top, and add a sticker or written message, if desired.

Cold-Weather Collection

Pull winterwear out from drawers and display them as part of your seasonal decor. If knit mittens don't have hangers, make a simple crocheted chain or use yarn.

Cableknit Wraps

In keeping with the knit theme, make wrapping papers that blend right in. Simply photocopy knit items and use the copies as gift wrap.

Hoop Happy

Miniature embroidery hoops transform old sweater remnants into festive wall hangings or ornaments. Place 3-inch embroidery hoops over display-worthy areas of a sweater; tighten. Cut out, trim as needed, and hang with ribbon.

Homespun-Style Stockings

Santa may want to slip these booties over his chilled toes! To make a stocking, turn a sweater inside out and pin any simple stocking pattern over an interesting part of the sweater design. Cut out stocking front and back. Use a zigzag stitch all around, leaving the top open. Trim any excess fabric along seams. Turn right side out. Hot-glue a length of sweater ribbon to form the cuff of the stocking. For a hanger, braid a length of yarn and knot it to measure about 5 inches, then sew ends in place at top back of stocking.

Dancing Stars Garland

Cut star shapes from sweater fabric. Adhere heavy iron-on fusible interfacing to the backs of the stars; trim. Hot-glue a large sequin in the center of each star, then glue to yarn.

Soft and Cushy

Wonderful second-hand sweaters bring pattern and style to traditional pillow shapes. Adhere iron-on fusible interfacing to the back of rectangles cut from sweaters. Sew pillows, leaving an opening to turn. Stuff with fiberfill and sew openings closed.

Leg Warmers

Cut the arms from sweaters in half lengthwise and sew a seam in each to create tubes to fit stool legs. Turn ends under 1 inch and hem. Slide onto legs.

Toasty Treasures
Give everyday candles and clear vases a cozy wrap. Cut off the end of a sweater arm to a length that fits container, plus about 2 inches. Fold the edge under and fasten it with hot glue. Glue on miniature jingle bells for festive flair.

Blue Christmas

Grace your home with a snow-kissed scene of blue that is fitting for the entire winter season.

Wintry Window Catcher

Skates are a natural addition to seasonal decor and this pair is spectacular. Fill with greenery, pinecones, and miniature ornaments hot-glued into place. Plentiful bows complete the elegant arrangement.

Gazing Ball Bliss

Traditionally found in a garden, reflecting summer sun, gazing balls make a big impact placed centerstage on the table. To steady them, place each ball on a grapevine wreath that has been brushed with white paint and sprinkled with artificial snow. Battery-operated snowflake lights offer added glow.

Jingle Bell Twist

Trim glasses in a jiffy using a wired sprig of artificial greenery. For a focal point, thread three jingle bells onto wire, wrap around stem, and clip off excess

Snow-Laden Ring

Miniature grapevine wreaths are just the right size to step in as napkin rings. To add a frosty look, brush with a light coat of white acrylic paint.

Fallen Flake

Salad plates get in on the theme with single snowflakes landing on each plate. To make one, cut a snowflake to fit using printer paper; iron flat. Attach the cutout to the back of a clear glass plate using double sided tape. In a well-ventilated work area, spray the plate back with silver paint; let dry then remove cutout.

Festive Flurry

Make art pieces as unique as snowflakes. Cut out a trio of paper snowflakes; iron flat and set aside. Using a wide foam paintbrush and "X" strokes, cover the front and sides of artist's canvas with shades of blue, white, and silver as shown in Photo A. Let paint dry. Arrange snowflakes on canvas. Spray canvas with random puffs of white paint, allowing some areas of blue to show as shown in Photo B. When dry, add very light random puffs of silver paint, as shown in Photo C. When dry, remove snowflakes, as shown in Photo D.

Candy Landing

A grapevine nest, from a crafts store, makes a fun holder for a candy dish. Brush the top of the nest with white acrylic paint then sprinkle with artificial snow to create a wintry effect. Line the nest with a clear glass dish before filling with wrapped candies.

Distressed Star

If you love plaid, this front-door star lets you strut a beautiful sampling. Use a metal star for the base. For each spoke, fold plaid paper over the star and cut to fit. Fold down the center to make aligning easy. To distress paper, lightly rub using medium-grit sandpaper. Adhere papers to the star using a glue stick. For a polished look, hot-glue oversized chenille stem trim around the edges and in crevices where papers meet.

Plaid O' Plenty

From the trims on the tree to the mantel and table, plaid reigns in this cozy Christmas decorating style.

Mix 'n' Match

Keep the color palette minimal and a variety of plaids will be more than compatible—they will complement each other. This display uses traditional Christmas colors, but you can choose whatever blends with your decor.

Daring Display

From rink to table, this clever duo
screams winter fun. To use as a tabletop
decoration, protect table with glass cut to
size. Replace laces with plaid ribbon
tipped with wood beads. Add greenery and
lollipops to complete the presentation.
Prop with an easel or gift-wrapped brick.

Star Players

Just like the front-door version on page 54, these small stars elicit big impact. Make them using cardboard stars as bases. Cover each spoke with plaid paper using glue stick to secure. Hot-glue chenille stems around outer edges.

Bough Bow

Achieve a decorator look with this thrifty trim. Make a trio of loops with wide wire-edge ribbon; secure ends with wire and tuck into tree.

Nesting In

Invite feathered friends to nestle in your tree. Dust the top of nest with white acrylic paint followed with glitter; let dry. Place an artificial bird in the nest. Hot-glue a berry pick and ribbon bow to the back.

Too Cute

Here's a no-sew tree skirt that cushions gifts with country style. Cut desired size tree skirt from plaid fabric. To finish the edge, use quick-set fabric glue to attach wide contrasting rickrack.

Ready to Receive

Whether different or matching, plaid stockings add country charm to holiday decorating. Use any basic stocking pattern to make stockings and use contrasting fabric for the cuff. For the grand finale, cover two large button forms with the stocking fabric and sew to the cuff for a striking accent.

Tartan Trims

Large tagboard snowflakes, covered with plaid paper, transform a plain wreath into one with striking style. Trace around snowflakes on the right side of plaid paper; cut out. Use a glue stick to adhere cutouts to snowflakes. Hot-glue silver chenille stems around all edges, piecing to cover entire edge.

Very Vintage

Magazine covers from years gone by make exciting conversation pieces. Check flea markets and antique stores for winter covers that blend with your decorating colors. Using triple mats allows you to frame the image in two plaids, separating with crisp white. To cover the mats, cut strips from wrapping paper to fit, mitering corners. Glue stick holds the pieces in place. To distress, gently rub with medium-grit sandpaper.

Time Worn

This fun flea-market find, an antique pair of child's skis, brings interest to the hearth. Cross the skis and fasten with wire. To bundle greenery and pinecone picks, wrap with wire. Wire the bundle to the skis and tie a large plaid ribbon bow at the top.

Under Wraps

Create merry spheres to display in a bed of greenery. The disguised plastic foam balls are wrapped with lengths of plaid fabric that has been cut or torn into strips. Straight pins hold the ends in place.

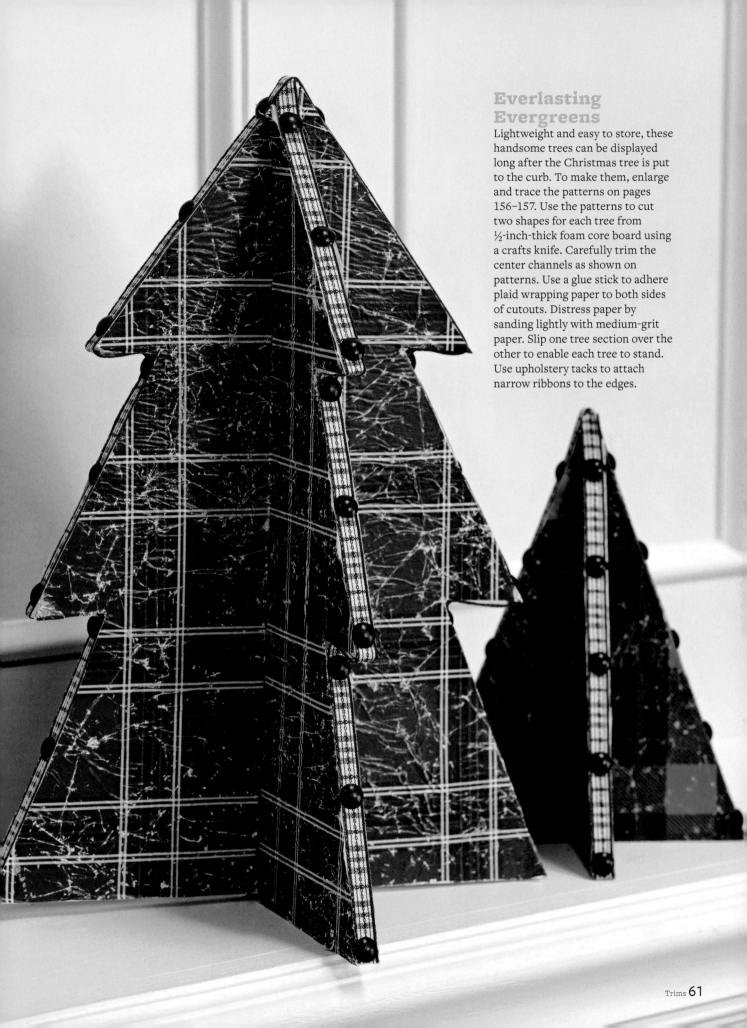

Everlasting Evergreens

Lightweight and easy to store, these handsome trees can be displayed long after the Christmas tree is put to the curb. To make them, enlarge and trace the patterns on pages 156–157. Use the patterns to cut two shapes for each tree from ½-inch-thick foam core board using a crafts knife. Carefully trim the center channels as shown on patterns. Use a glue stick to adhere plaid wrapping paper to both sides of cutouts. Distress paper by sanding lightly with medium-grit paper. Slip one tree section over the other to enable each tree to stand. Use upholstery tacks to attach narrow ribbons to the edges.

Party Ready

Solid red and white accents allow the various plaids on the tabletop to shine. Candlelight adds to the coziness.

Nice Touch

Candles get in on the plaid act when wrapped with wide ribbon. Attach to candle using straight pins. For safety, affix ribbon well below wick.

Sleigh Bells Ring

Chairs get a grand adornment inspired by Santa himself. To mimic the look of sleigh bells, cut 14-inch lengths from inexpensive black belts with side-by-side eyelets. To get the most for your money, purchase long belts so you can make two or three chair trims from each. Attach three large silver jingle bells to each belt strip using short lengths of silver chenille stems. Fold top of belt over chair and use another chenille stem to secure the loop and hold the trim to the chair. Tie a large plaid ribbon bow to the top of the trim.

Quick Coaster

Laser-cut snowflakes make great seasonal coasters. Paint the tops white and let dry. Several layers of clear topcoat (allowing to dry between coats) protect the wood from moisture.

Seasonal Swap

If chair seats are fabric and detach easily, wrap a plaid cloth napkin or fabric piece around cushion and reattach to chair. If chairs have wood seats, sew simple chair seat pads using plaid fabrics.

Fast Favors

Enhance favor cups with a narrow plaid bow topped with a laser-cut wood snowflake and a press-on gem. To plaid it up even more, line each cup with a square of plaid tissue paper.

Silver & Gold Glitz

Pair silver and gold for a ritzy approach to holiday decorating.

Sparkling Surprise Holders

Cardboard tubes hold tiny treasures for everyone gathered around the holiday table. To make the surprise holders, use bathroom tissue rolls or paper towel tubes trimmed to size. Cut metallic gold wrapping paper large enough to wrap tube, extending 4 inches beyond tube ends. Tape together at seam. Cut a piece of matching glitter paper, trimmed 1 inch shorter than tube, and tack in place with dots of hot glue. Wrap tube with a short length of ribbon, securing ends with a large press-on decorative gem. Carefully pinch one end of wrapping paper just beyond end of tube; tie with ribbon. Fill tube with small items, such as candy, toys, and confetti. Pinch and tie up remaining end.

14-Karat Candies

Miniature candy bars gain swank with the addition of a snippet of ribbon and a press-on button. Choose candy bars with an underwrap of gold or silver; remove outer wrap. Cut a short length of ribbon to wrap around candy; hot-glue ends in place. Adhere a press-on button to ribbon.

Seasonal Salutations

Silver, gold, and black unite to make a striking framed piece. Use stickers and rub-on letters to display wintry and holiday words. Use varying fonts, sizes, and placement to achieve an eclectic look.

Glam Glasses

Make happy hour one to remember with gorgeous silver and gold trims adorning stemware. Wrap each stem with a small pick and wired clear beads (often found with wedding embellishments in crafts stores). Tie a double bow at the base using narrow silver and gold ribbon

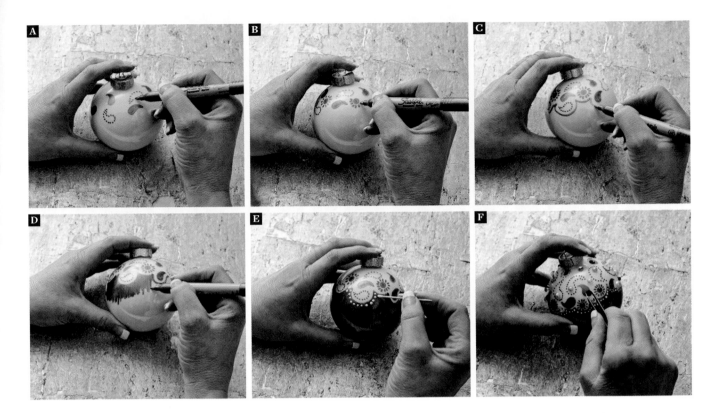

Paisleys and Polka-Dots

Totally glamorous and one of a kind, these elegant ornaments are made easily using a marking pen and press-on embellishments. Using a permanent gold marking pen on a white ornament, draw dotted and colored-in paisley shapes around the top, as shown in Photo A. Fill in between paisleys with small dots encircled with short rays, as shown in Photo B. Leaving a narrow border, draw a line just below the designs, as shown in Photo C. Color in the bottom, as shown in Photo D. Let dry thoroughly. Using a toothpick and white gloss acrylic paint, make dots along the gold edge, as shown in Photo E. Use tweezers to place adhesive acrylic gems and pearls on ornament, as shown in Photo F.

One for All

Here's a fun tradition that gets everyone in the holiday spirit. When company arrives, let them find their initial ornaments and hang them on the tree. When you admire your tree in the days that follow, you'll smile, recalling happy holiday memories.

Wooden Wonders

With a little TLC, unfinished wooden shapes transform into handsome holiday trims.

Easy Accents

Laser-cut snowflakes are lovely as is, but add a light coat of stain and upholstery tack heads and the lacy ornaments become even prettier. To enrich the surface, wipe with a coat of medium stain and let dry. Wearing protective glasses, use a wire cutter to clip off the heads of decorative tacks. Uniformly place and hot-glue heads to snowflake.

Focal Point

Wooden sled miniatures, which are common finds during the winter season, bring old-fashioned charm to the tree. Spruce them up with a coat of stain and a metal embellishment glued in the center. To hang, cut heads off two upholstery tacks, leaving a short length of nail. Poke nail through one end of a 6-inch-long piece of ribbon, add a drop of hot glue, and press into one side of sled runner; repeat on opposite side.

Trim a Tree

No one will know these sweet trees are usually found in the kitchen. Wooden cone rollers work perfectly as Christmas tree ornaments. Enliven the wood with a coat of stain and let dry. Use a hammer to tap upholstery tacks around the lower edge, shown. To hang, twist a screw eye in the top and tie with a ribbon bow.

Tack It Down

Wooden balls, available in crafts stores, require little finishing to make them into ornaments. Wipe on a coat of stain to bring out the grain; let dry. Use a hammer to nail upholstery tacks through narrow ribbon and into the ball, as shown, adding evenly spaced tacks to hold the ribbon in place. For hanging, twist a screw eye in the top and tie with a ribbon bow. Thread with wire or cord for hanging.

Big Ideas, Small Spaces

When downsizing is the name of the game, there's no reason to give up wonderful holiday decorations. These festive trees take minimal space.

Pallet Pine

Repurpose a large wooden shipping pallet—often available free at hardware or garden supply stores—and create a charming card display. To make it, draw a large triangle on a pallet (this example is 44 inches tall). Choose an area that has a vertical support for the horizontal slats. Cut out the triangle using a jigsaw; use sandpaper to smooth surfaces. Paint tree slats with alternative shades of green. Predrill holes, then screw small cup hooks and drawer pulls to the front. Tie rope between knobs; attach clothespins to rope. Display with cards, ornaments, and more.

Candy Crush

Tiered strings of candy canes sweeten a kid's room. Cut twine to four different lengths; the longest approximately 26 inches. Tie on canes, spacing them 2 inches apart. Tack or tape ends to secure.

Family Tree

Old photos are typical conversation starters, particularly during the holidays, and this display takes up minimal wall space. Cut baby photographs in circles, mount on foam core, and arrange in a tree shape. Keep paper name tags in a bowl and have family members guess who's who. Pin up guesses with ball-head pins.

Mirror, Mirror On the Wall

YOU will be the fairest of them all with this quick and clever seasonal touch. In a well-ventilated work area, cover surface with newspaper. Spray an unframed mirror with artificial snow spray and draw a simple Christmas tree into the snow using your finger. The artificial snow will wash off when the season ends so the mirror can be put to use when the tree goes down.

Picture This

Gather your favorite collectible ornaments and trim the boughs of a whimsical art piece. Hung inside a frame topped with a bow, the ornaments are the center of attention.

WHAT YOU NEED

Black crafts wire in 16-gauge and 20-gauge
Wire cutter
Pliers
Jewelry pliers
Ornaments
Wood frame, sized to fit around the tree
Glue gun and hot-glue adhesive

Glittery star ornament with hanging loop
Ribbon bow

WHAT YOU DO

1. Determine the size of wire tree desired by drawing a triangle on paper and testing the spacing of the boughs in relation to the ornaments to be displayed. This tree is about 15 inches tall and 10½ inches wide at the bottom.
2. For the tree, form a triangle from the 16-gauge wire. Use pliers to twist the wire ends together at top. For boughs, cut four pieces of wire slightly wider than the triangle, allowing about an inch overhang to curl the ends.

3. Attach boughs, twisting each wire end around the side of the tree, then using the jewelry pliers to curl the ends.
4. Cut small pieces of 20-gauge wire for ornament hooks. Use jewelry pliers to shape the wire pieces into S-shape ornament holders. Hang the wire tree on the wall.
5. Attach S-shape holders to ornaments and hang them from the wire boughs. Hot-glue the star ornament and ribbon bow to the top center of the frame.
6. Hang the frame, centering the wire tree within the frame so the star appears to be the tree topper.

Wall Tower

This may just be the best thing since artificial trees—a wall-mounted Christmas "tree" that takes up little space and doesn't shed needles or require assembly. Hang small matching shelves in a triangle pattern on the wall then top each shelf with a different ensemble of Christmas decor favorites. Place a greenery-filled urn at the base for the tree "trunk" and surround with pretty wrapped presents.

Snapshot Moments

Somewhere in a shoebox or on a hard drive are images that will kindle family ties just in time for the holiday season. Give those memories more exposure with photo projects sprinkled throughout your home.

Soft Focus

Cushy and clever, this pillow touts a black-and-white photo for vintage appeal. To make the picture pillow, print a test of the photo onto white paper, selecting "mirror image" or "reverse image." Print black-and-white or color photo onto fabric transfer paper, following package instructions. If the photo is larger than 8½×11 inches, tape two pieces of transfer paper together on the reverse side before printing. Cut out image, leaving a narrow border. Place facedown on pillow cover, carefully remove any tape, then iron. Insert pillow form.

Simple shapes transform photos into quick ornaments and gift tags. Back with colored cardstock and trim narrow borders using plain or decorative-edge scissors. Adhere with glue stick and these mementos are ready to hang.

Dish Up Smiles

Evoke the best family memories with personalized plates. Size a photo to fit the flat area of a glass plate. Print photo onto vellum, seal with polyacrylic spray, and cut to fit. Using a foam brush, coat underside of plate with decoupage medium; place photo and smooth. Let dry. Apply two more coats of decoupage medium to vellum, letting dry between coats. Hand-wash only.

Open Case

Back a seasonal arrangement with a favorite wintertime image. Secure an enlarged photo with double-sided tape inside the lid of a vintage-style suitcase or lunch box. Fill container with apples, pinecones, and greenery.

Word Play

Display a meaningful message. Paint fiberboard letters; let dry. Arrange photos over O, taping together with low-tack tape. Carefully flip photos and letter facedown and trace around O. Remove letter; cut photos along lines. Adhere photos to letter with decoupage medium. Remove tape.

Clearly Creative

Let tabletop containers tell stories of days past through the use of photographs. Gently roll and insert photocopies into glass vessels. Add sprigs and twine for casual appeal.

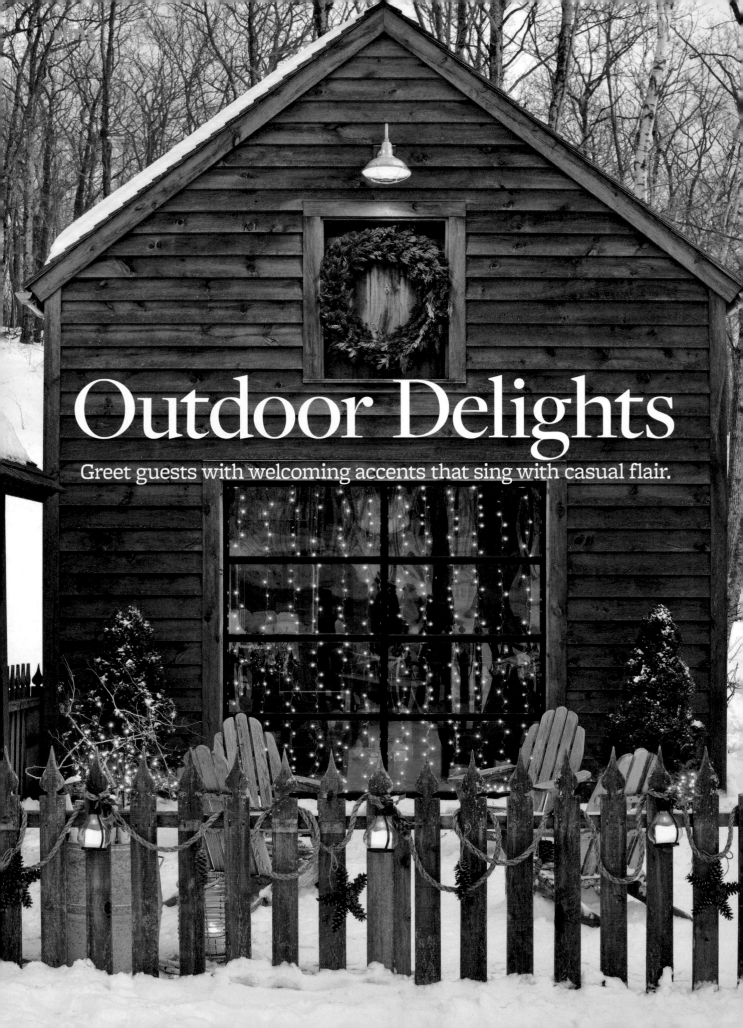

Outdoor Delights

Greet guests with welcoming accents that sing with casual flair.

Rustic Garland

Decorate a fence by casually looping ¾-inch manila rope through the pickets. Tie on pinecone stars, flameless lanterns, and fresh holly sprigs for cheer. The stars add seasonal shapes while keeping beautifully organic. To make them, hot-glue ends of five pinecones to a 4-inch cardboard disc, leaving a small space in the center for five tiny pinecones and a single floret.

O Tannenbaum

Spruce up any live evergreen by tying pinecones to branches with jute twine and placing a pinecone star on top. Ring the base with a skirt of dancing flames made with galvanized metal pails spray-painted festive red. Fill with snow (or sand), glass chimneys, and pillar candles. If you do not have live trees, prop a 5-foot-tall balsam fir in a tree stand as shown here.

Light Display

Lights make just about anything inviting. A few lights draped over a branch propped up with birch logs in a time-worn barrel give off a radiant glow.

Ah, Natural

Pre-lit branches make a festive addition to a planter awaiting spring. Nestle in a few large pinecones to enhance the display.

Sign of the Time

Spread the word! The message on this chalkboard sign lasts a long time, thanks to a coat of clear sealer. To make your own cheery sign, paint a piece of plywood with red chalkboard paint; then use white chalk to letter the surface. In a well-ventilated work area, spray board with clear sealer. Frame the board as desired.

Gal-Pal New Year Party

Ring in the New Year with party favors, glass charms, and table decorations that are especially themed for a very special girls' night out.

Fun Frills

A mob of curling ribbon in pink and silver adds festive flair to the front door. To create the wreath, wrap a flat wreath form with glittered ribbon. To make the adornment, cover a cardboard cone with art paper and hot-glue trim to the rim. Cut approximately twenty 72-inch-long lengths of curling ribbon; knot together in center. Use scissors to curl the ribbon ends. Tape the center knot inside the cone. Hot-glue house numbers, signifying the new year, to the bottom of the wreath.

Great Grate

Visit home improvement stores to find an array of patterned aluminum sheets. Layer a die-cut version over a solid aluminum piece. Dress up the tone-on-tone metal mat with ribbons wrapped around the layers and taped to the back side.

Elegant Lighting

Give glass votive candleholders the wow factor with the addition of ribbons and adhesive gems and embellishments. For safety, keep all embellishments below the rim of the candleholders.

Pretty in Pink Favors

Number stickers, in the same color as the pail, make a sophisticated statement. Tie a contrasting ribbon bow to the handle and fill with goodies.

Serving Tray Bling

A rectangular duct cap reflects color and light for a glitzy effect. This duct work piece does just that as it goes to work as a serving tray. To add dazzle, add a sticker gem initial along with acrylic gem clusters and a glittered cutout in one corner.

Glass Class

Personalized glass charms help guests keep track of their beverages. To make the initial tag, use a circle punch to cut a shape from silver cardstock. Apply a sticker letter embellished with a gem. Use a paper punch to make a hole at the top and attach to glass stem with ball chain. For quick coasters, use 4-inch vent caps and trim with adhesive gem strips.

Clever Combo

No one would guess this ruffle-edged holder is actually a 3-inch storm collar. Line it with a glass bowl and it becomes a serving dish for party snacks.

In-A-Twinkling
Festive Favors

Merry Miniatures

Darling and diminutive, these bottlebrush tree arrangements deliver a big dose of holiday cheer. Hot-glue a ribbon bow to the top of each tree; glue base to a tiny glass dish. Edge the rim with trim then, in one corner, add miniature ornaments topped with a jingle bell.

Wrapped and Ready to Glow

Dollar store candles look like boutique buys with a couple quick decorative touches. Wrap each glass candleholder with silver and red cording; hot-glue ends to candleholder to secure. Tie a cord bow and glue in center of wraps. Glue mini pinecones and artificial berries just above the bow.

One to Grow With

Have a group of gardening friends? They'll be singing your praises when they take home little starter pots. Use an awl to poke two holes on one side of a cardboard planter; tie with cord. Fill the container with bulbs, seeds, and an ornament or two for some holiday cheer.

Cookie Stacks

Foil-wrapped cookies, purchased or wrapped yourself, already look celebratory. But stacked, tied with a bow, and accented with an artificial sprig of holly, these little sweets are downright favor worthy. To make bow tying easy, place a small piece of double-sided tape between layers when stacking.

Shabby Chic

Quaint envelopes wrap CDs and other surprises with flair. Trim paper to size, using one piece for front, back, and flap. Trim flap using decorative-edge scissors. Place white cardstock under flap, machine sew along edge, and trim. Fold envelope and stitch sides. Tie thread through a button; hot-glue to flap.

Festive Frill

A plain pail gets dressed up for the holidays with the simple addition of feather boa and a pair of glittered jingle bells. Hot-glue the trims to the pail, line with tissue paper, and fill the pretty container with holiday cookies or candies.

GINGERBREAD CAKE ROLL
recipe on page 104

food

THE HOLIDAY TABLE

GATHER

Bring family and friends to the table to indulge in foods that are truly once-a-year treats. Sweet and savory party nibbles, a mix-and-match feast, easy-on-the cook sides, and a selection of holiday pies make the season special.

GIANDUJA MOUSSE CAKE
recipe on page 104

CHERRY PINWHEELS
recipe on page 94

Festive Finger Foods

A selection of sweet and savory nibbles that can be neatly eaten with your hands makes perfect party food.

CHEESE AND
VEGETABLE STRUDEL
recipe on page 94

Cherry Pinwheels

(Shown on page 92.)

WHAT YOU NEED

½ cup butter, softened
1 cup granulated sugar
1 teaspoon baking powder
¼ teaspoon baking soda
   Dash salt
½ cup sour cream
1 egg
1 teaspoon lemon zest
1 teaspoon vanilla
2¾ cups all-purpose flour
¾ cup cherry preserves
1 cup powdered sugar
¼ teaspoon almond extract
3 to 4 teaspoons milk

WHAT YOU DO

1. In a large mixing bowl beat butter with an electric mixer on medium to high speed for 30 seconds. Add granulated sugar, baking powder, baking soda, and salt. Beat until combined, scraping sides of bowl occasionally. Beat in sour cream, egg, lemon zest, and vanilla until combined. Beat in as much of the flour as you can with the mixer. Stir in any remaining flour. Divide dough into four equal portions. Cover and chill dough about 2 hours or until easy to handle.
2. Preheat oven to 375°F. Line cookie sheets with parchment paper; set aside. On a lightly floured surface roll one portion of the dough at a time into a 7½-inch square. Using a straight or fluted pastry wheel, cut dough into 2½-inch squares. (Keep remaining dough chilled. If dough becomes too soft, return to refrigerator for a few minutes).
3. Place squares 2 inches apart on the prepared cookie sheets. Using the pastry wheel, cut 1-inch slits from corners toward the center of each square. Snip any large pieces of fruit in the preserves. Spoon 1 level teaspoon of the preserves into the center of each square. Fold each tip to the center to form a pinwheel. Press the dough gently in center to seal tips to the filling.
4. Bake for 8 to 9 minutes or just until edges begin to brown. Cool on cookie sheet for 3 minutes. Transfer cookies to a wire rack and let cool.
5. For icing, in a small bowl stir together powdered sugar, almond extract, and enough milk to make icing drizzling consistency. Drizzle over cooled cookies. Let stand until set. Makes 36 cookies.

Cheese and Vegetable Strudel

A warm, flaky slice of this veggie-and-cheese-filled pastry is a delicious accompaniment to a glass of chilled white wine.

WHAT YOU NEED

1 10-ounce package frozen chopped spinach, thawed, well drained, and squeezed dry
1 cup crumbled feta cheese (4 ounces)
¾ cup chopped red sweet pepper (1 medium)
2 ounces semisoft cheese with garlic and fine herbes or soft goat cheese (chèvre)
⅓ cup pine nuts, toasted
¼ cup chopped onion
2 tablespoons snipped fresh basil and/or chives
2 tablespoons finely chopped, drained oil-packed dried tomatoes
2 cloves garlic, minced
12 sheets frozen phyllo dough (14×9-inch rectangles), thawed
⅓ cup butter, melted

WHAT YOU NEED

1. Preheat oven to 375°F. Line a 15×10×1-inch baking pan with parchment paper; set aside. For filling, in a bowl combine spinach, feta cheese, sweet pepper, semisoft cheese, pine nuts, onion, basil, dried tomatoes, and garlic.
2. Unroll phyllo dough. Place one sheet of phyllo on a work surface. (While you work, keep the remaining phyllo covered with plastic wrap to prevent it from drying out.) Brush phyllo sheet with some of the melted butter. Top with five more phyllo sheets, brushing each sheet with melted butter.
3. Spread half the filling on phyllo stack to within ½ inch of the edges. From a short edge, roll up phyllo, folding in sides as you roll. Place roll, seam side down, in the prepared baking pan. Brush top with melted butter. Repeat with remaining phyllo, melted butter, and filling.
4. Bake for 23 to 25 minutes or until phyllo is golden and filling is heated through. Cool in pan on a wire rack for 10 minutes. Cut into slices. Serve warm. Makes about 20 servings.

Hazelnut Shortbread Sandwich Cookies

There are ground hazelnuts in the shortbread and chocolate-hazelnut spread in the center of these buttery bites.

WHAT YOU NEED

2 cups all-purpose flour
1 cup hazelnuts, chopped
½ teaspoon salt
1 cup unsalted butter, softened
¾ cup powdered sugar
½ cup chocolate-hazelnut spread
2 to 4 tablespoons whipping cream
   White baking chocolate with cocoa butter, melted (optional)

WHAT YOU DO

1. In a food processor combine flour, ½ cup of the hazelnuts, and the salt. Cover and process about 1 minute or until nuts are finely ground. Transfer flour mixture to a medium bowl. In the processor combine butter and powdered sugar. Cover and process until smooth. Add flour mixture. Cover and process with on/off pulses just until a dough forms, scraping down sides of bowl as necessary. Add the remaining ½ cup hazelnuts. Cover and process with on/off pulses until combined. Divide dough in half. Shape each half into an 8-inch roll. Wrap each roll in plastic wrap or waxed paper. Freeze 30 minutes or until firm.
2. Preheat oven to 350°F. Line a large cookie sheet with parchment paper. Cut rolls into ¼-inch slices. Place slices 1 inch apart on cookie sheet. Bake for 12 to 15 minutes or just until edges are golden. Cool on cookie sheet on a wire rack.
3. For ganache, in a small microwave-safe bowl microwave the chocolate-hazelnut spread on 100 percent power (high) about 1 minute or until warm, stirring once. Stir 2 tablespoons of the whipping cream into the chocolate-hazelnut spread. If necessary, stir in additional whipping cream, a small amount at a time, to reach spreading consistency.
4. Spread 1 teaspoon of the ganache onto bottoms of half the cookies. Top with the remaining cookies, bottom sides down. Decorate sandwich cookies with the remaining ganache (thin with additional whipping cream if necessary) and, if desired, melted white chocolate. Makes 25 sandwich cookies.

HAZELNUT SHORTBREAD
SANDWICH COOKIES

PEPPERONI PIZZA CUPS

Pepperoni Pizza Cups

Kids and adults alike will dig into these mini pizzas baked in muffin cups. If you're having a big crowd, make a double batch—one each of the pepperoni and Italian sausage or vegetarian versions (see Tip, below).

WHAT YOU NEED

1 pound frozen pizza dough, thawed
   Cornmeal
1 cup pasta sauce
2 teaspoons dried oregano, crushed
2 cups shredded mozzarella or cheddar cheese (8 ounces)
½ 3.5-ounce package sliced pepperoni, chopped
¼ cup finely shredded Parmesan cheese (1 ounce)
   Snipped fresh oregano (optional)

WHAT YOU DO

1. Let dough stand at room temperature for 15 minutes. Preheat oven to 375°F. Grease twelve 2½-inch muffin cups; coat cups lightly with cornmeal. Set aside.
2. On a lightly floured surface roll dough into a 16×12-inch rectangle. If dough is difficult to roll, let it rest for a few minutes as necessary during rolling. Using a sharp knife or pizza cutter, cut into twelve 4-inch squares. Lightly press dough squares into the prepared muffin cups, extending edges over rims of cups.
3. In a small bowl combine pasta sauce and dried oregano. Spread some of the sauce in dough-lined cups. Fill with mozzarella cheese and pepperoni. Top with the remaining sauce and sprinkle with the shredded Parmesan cheese.
4. Bake for 25 to 30 minutes or until crusts are golden. Cool in muffin cups on a wire rack for 5 minutes. Remove from muffin cups. If desired, sprinkle pizza cups with snipped fresh oregano. Serve warm. Makes 12 servings.
Tip: Cooked Italian sausage or chopped mushrooms and green sweet peppers can be substituted for the pepperoni.

PESTO CHICKEN PHYLLO STRAWS

Pesto Chicken Phyllo Straws

Serve these savory straws warm. Make them up to 8 hours ahead and just pop them in the oven right before your guests arrive.

WHAT YOU NEED

3 cups finely shredded or finely chopped rotisserie chicken
¼ cup purchased pesto sauce
⅓ cup finely shredded Parmesan cheese
20 sheets frozen phyllo dough (14×9-inch rectangles), thawed (half of a 16-ounce package)
½ cup butter, melted
1½ cups finely shredded Monterey Jack cheese

WHAT YOU DO

1. Preheat oven to 400°F. Line two baking sheets with parchment paper; set aside.
2. For filling, in a medium bowl stir together the chicken, pesto, and Parmesan cheese. Set aside.

3. With a very sharp knife cut the stack of phyllo sheets in half crosswise to make 40 rectangles (9×7 inches). Lightly brush one of the phyllo sheets with some of the melted butter. (Keep the remaining phyllo sheets covered with plastic wrap to prevent them from drying out.)
4. For each straw, sprinkle about 1 tablespoon of the filling in a strip ½ inch from one long side of the phyllo rectangle. Sprinkle filling with 1 teaspoon of the Monterey Jack cheese. Tightly roll up phyllo. Place straw, seam side down, on the prepared baking sheet; brush straw with a little more butter. Repeat with the remaining phyllo rectangles, filling, and cheese.
5. Bake for 12 to 15 minutes or until straws are golden brown and crisp. Serve warm. Makes 40 straws.
Make-Ahead Tip: If desired, loosely cover straws with plastic wrap. Cover and chill up to 8 hours. Bake as directed.

CAJUN TURKEY
SLIDERS WITH SPICY
REMOULADE

Cajun Turkey Sliders with Spicy Remoulade

WHAT YOU NEED

2   tablespoons vegetable oil
1   medium red sweet pepper, seeded and cut into thin strips
1   medium yellow sweet pepper, seeded and cut into thin strips
1   medium onion, cut into thin wedges
1½ pounds uncooked ground turkey
¼   cup chopped green onions
2   teaspoons Cajun seasoning
1   teaspoon bottled hot pepper sauce
½   teaspoon salt
¼   teaspoon ground black pepper
12 whole wheat cocktail buns, split and toasted
2   tablespoons Old Bay® seasoning
1   recipe Spicy Remoulade

WHAT YOU DO

1. In an extra-large skillet heat 1 tablespoon of the oil over medium-low heat. Add sweet peppers and onion; cook about 10 minutes or until very soft and tender. Remove from skillet; keep warm.
2. In a large bowl combine turkey, green onions, Cajun seasoning, bottled hot pepper sauce, salt, and black pepper; mix well. Form into 12 patties slightly larger than the buns. Sprinkle both sides of each patty generously with seasoning.
3. In the same skillet heat the remaining 1 tablespoon oil over medium heat. Add patties; cook about 8 minutes or until done (165°F), turning once halfway through cooking time.
4. Serve patties in buns with sweet peppers and Spicy Remoulade. Makes 12 sliders.

Spicy Remoulade: In a medium bowl combine 1 cup mayonnaise; ¼ cup pickle relish; 2 tablespoons capers, drained; 1 tablespoon Creole or spicy brown mustard; 1 tablespoon snipped fresh parsley; 2 teaspoons bottled hot pepper sauce; and 1 teaspoon lemon juice.

tip: The internal color of a burger is not a reliable doneness indicator. A poultry patty cooked to 165°F is safe, regardless of color. To measure the doneness of a patty, insert an instant-read thermometer through the side into the center of the patty.

PEANUT BUTTER TRUFFLES

Peanut Butter Truffles

Two favorite flavors come together in these easy-to-make treats. They can be made up to 2 weeks ahead and stored in the refrigerator.

WHAT YOU NEED

2   cups sugar
1   5-ounce can evaporated milk
½   cup butter
2   cups tiny marshmallows
¾   cup creamy peanut butter
½   teaspoon vanilla
12 ounces dark or bittersweet chocolate, chopped
2   teaspoons shortening
    Finely chopped peanuts (optional)

WHAT YOU DO

1. Butter the sides of a medium-size heavy saucepan. In the saucepan combine sugar, evaporated milk, and butter. Cook and stir over medium-high heat until boiling. Reduce heat to medium; continue boiling at a moderate, steady rate for 12 minutes, stirring occasionally.
2. Remove saucepan from heat. Stir in marshmallows, peanut butter, and vanilla. Transfer to a large bowl. Chill for 45 to 60 minutes or until peanut butter mixture is thick and can be molded.
3. Line a large baking sheet with waxed paper or parchment paper. Shape peanut butter mixture into 1-inch balls; place on the prepared baking sheet. Freeze for 15 minutes.
4. In a medium saucepan combine chocolate and shortening. Cook and stir over low heat until melted. Dip balls, one at a time, into melted chocolate. Let excess chocolate drip off balls. Place on a wire rack set over waxed paper. If desired, sprinkle with peanuts. Let stand until chocolate is set. Makes about 50 truffles.

Tip: If desired, when dark chocolate is set, drizzle with a little melted milk chocolate. Let stand until milk chocolate is set.

Make-Ahead Tip: Prepare as directed. Layer truffles between sheets of waxed paper in an airtight container; seal. Store in the refrigerator up to 2 weeks.

Mix & Match

Pick a main dish—roast turkey or stuffed pork tenderloin—then fill out the feast with a fabulous side or two and dessert.

GOLDEN ROASTED
TURKEY WITH PAN GRAVY

Golden Roasted Turkey with Pan Gravy

WHAT YOU NEED

1   10- to 12-pound turkey
3   tablespoons butter
2   tablespoons honey
2   teaspoons snipped fresh thyme
2   teaspoons snipped fresh rosemary
2   teaspoons snipped fresh sage
¼   teaspoon salt
¼   teaspoon ground black pepper
1½   cups low-sodium chicken broth
2   tablespoons all-purpose flour
2   oranges, cut into wedges
     and/or slices and lightly browned
     (optional)
     Fresh sage sprigs (optional)

WHAT YOU DO

1. Preheat oven to 325°F. Remove neck and giblets from turkey; reserve for another use or discard. Rinse turkey body cavity; pat dry with paper towels.
2. Skewer neck skin to back. Tuck drumstick ends under band of skin across tail (if present) or tie drumsticks to the tail using 100-percent-cotton kitchen string. Twist wing tips under back.
3. In a small saucepan combine butter, honey, thyme, rosemary, sage, salt, and pepper. Heat for 2 to 3 minutes or until butter is melted. Brush honey mixture over turkey, and, if desired, under skin on breast. Insert an oven-going meat thermometer into center of an inside thigh muscle (thermometer should not touch bone). Cover loosely with foil.
4. Roast turkey for 2¼ hours. Remove foil; roast for 30 to 45 minutes more (60 to 75 minutes if stuffed) or until the meat thermometer registers at least 175°F in the thigh; if stuffed the center of the stuffing must register 165°F. Drumsticks should move easily in their sockets. Remove turkey from oven. Cover with foil; let stand for 15 to 20 minutes before carving.
5. For pan gravy, strain pan drippings into a fat separator. In a small saucepan combine ½ cup of the defatted juices and 2 tablespoons of the turkey fat. Whisk in chicken broth and flour. Bring to boiling over medium-high heat. Cook for 3 minutes. If desired, garnish turkey with oranges and sage sprigs. Serve turkey with gravy. Makes 12 servings.

APPLE, BACON, AND LEEK DRESSING

Apple, Bacon, and Leek Dressing

WHAT YOU NEED

     Nonstick cooking spray
9   slices bacon
¼   cup butter
2   cups sliced fresh button
     mushrooms
1½   cups coarsely chopped leeks
1½   cups chopped celery (3 stalks)
3   cups coarsely chopped, peeled
     (if desired) Fuji or Granny Smith
     apples
6   cloves garlic, minced
½   cup whipping cream
12   cups dry country-style bread
     cubes*
1   tablespoon fresh snipped sage or
     1 teaspoon dried sage, crushed
1   tablespoon fresh thyme or
     1 teaspoon dried thyme, crushed
¼   teaspoon ground black pepper
1¼ to 1¾ cups chicken broth

WHAT YOU DO

1. Preheat oven to 350°F. Coat a 3-quart rectangular baking dish with cooking spray; set aside. In an extra-large skillet cook bacon over medium heat until crisp.

Remove bacon and drain on paper towels, reserving 3 tablespoons drippings in skillet. Crumble bacon; set aside. Add butter to reserved drippings. Add mushrooms, leeks, and celery. Cook over medium heat for 7 to 10 minutes or until vegetables are tender, stirring occasionally. Add apples and garlic. Cook and for 2 to 4 minutes or just until apples are softened. Stir in whipping cream.
2. In an extra-large bowl combine apple mixture, crumbled bacon, bread cubes, snipped or dried sage, thyme, and pepper. Drizzle with enough broth to moisten, tossing gently to combine. Transfer dressing to prepared baking dish.
3. Bake, uncovered, for 30 to 35 minutes or until heated through and top is lightly browned. Makes 12 servings.

Tip: To make dry bread cubes, preheat oven to 300°F. Cut 18 to 21 fresh bread slices into ½-inch cubes to yield 12 cups bread cubes. Spread cubes in two 15×10×1-inch baking pans. Bake for 10 to 15 minutes or until cubes are dry, stirring twice; cool. (Cubes will continue to dry and crisp as they cool.) Or let bread cubes stand, loosely covered, at room temperature for 8 to 12 hours.

FRUIT-FILLED PORK
TENDERLOIN

Fruit-Filled Pork Tenderloin

WHAT YOU NEED

½ cup ruby port wine
¾ cup golden raisins
¾ cup dried cranberries
⅔ cup dried apricots, quartered
¼ teaspoon apple pie spice
2 14- to 18-ounce pork tenderloins
½ teaspoon salt
¼ teaspoon ground black pepper

WHAT YOU DO

1. For filling, in a small saucepan bring port just to boiling. Remove from heat. Stir in raisins, dried cranberries, dried apricots, and apple pie spice. Cover and let stand for 15 minutes. Transfer mixture to a food processor. Cover and process for 10 to 15 seconds or until very coarsely chopped.
2. Preheat oven to 425°F. Make a lengthwise cut along the center of each tenderloin, cutting almost to but not through the other side. Spread open. Place each tenderloin between two pieces of plastic wrap. Using the flat side of a meat mallet, pound meat lightly from center to edges to slightly less than ½-inch thickness. Remove plastic wrap.
3. Divide fruit filling between meat portions, spreading to within ½ inch of edges. From a long side, roll each portion. Tie at 2-inch intervals with 100-percent-cotton kitchen string. Sprinkle rolls with salt and pepper.
4. Place tenderloin rolls on a rack in a shallow roasting pan. Roast for 25 to 35 minutes or until juices run clear and an instant-read thermometer inserted into meat registers 155°F. Remove from oven. Cover loosely with foil; let stand for 10 minutes. (Meat temperature after standing should be 160°F.)
5. Remove and discard string. Cut tenderloins into ½-inch slices. Makes 8 servings.

Green Beans with Shallots, Thyme, and Shiitake Mushrooms

WHAT YOU NEED

2 pounds green beans, trimmed
2 tablespoons olive oil
2 tablespoons butter
¼ cup thinly sliced shallots (2 medium)

GREEN BEANS WITH SHALLOTS, THYME, AND SHIITAKE MUSHROOMS

SPICE-AND-HONEY ROASTED CARROTS

12 ounces fresh shiitake mushrooms, stemmed and halved
2 teaspoons finely shredded lemon peel
3 tablespoons lemon juice
2 tablespoons fresh thyme
   Coarse sea salt or kosher salt
   Freshly ground black pepper
½ cup slivered almonds (optional)

WHAT YOU DO

1. In a large pot cook beans in enough lightly salted boiling water to cover for 8 to 10 minutes or until crisp-tender; drain. Transfer beans to a large bowl of ice water to halt cooking.
2. In an extra-large skillet heat oil and butter over medium heat. Add shallots; cook just until tender, stirring frequently. Add mushrooms; cook for 6 to 8 minutes or until tender, stirring frequently.
3. Add green beans; cook for 5 to 8 minutes or until heated through, tossing occasionally. Add lemon peel, lemon juice, and thyme; toss to combine. Season to taste with salt and pepper. If desired, sprinkle with almonds. Makes 8 servings.

Spice-and-Honey Roasted Carrots

WHAT YOU NEED

1½ pounds regular or tricolor carrots
1 tablespoon olive oil
½ cup coarsely chopped hazelnuts or almonds
1 tablespoon coriander seeds (optional)
1 tablespoon sesame seeds (optional)

1½ teaspoons cumin seeds (optional)
½ teaspoon salt
¼ teaspoon ground black pepper
1 tablespoon honey

WHAT YOU DO

1. Preheat oven to 425°F. Trim carrots, reserving tops if desired. Scrub carrots; if desired, peel carrots. Halve any large carrots lengthwise.
2. Line a shallow roasting pan with foil. Evenly spread carrots in the prepared roasting pan. Drizzle with olive oil. Roast carrots, uncovered, for 20 minutes.
3. Meanwhile, heat a small dry skillet over medium-high heat. Add hazelnuts; cook and stir about 3 minutes or until fragrant and toasted. Transfer to a bowl. If desired, add coriander seeds, sesame seeds, and cumin seeds to hot skillet. Cook over medium-high heat about 2 minutes or until fragrant and toasted. Remove spices from heat and transfer to another bowl; cool for 10 minutes.
4. Using a spice grinder, coffee grinder, or mortar and pestle, grind or crush toasted spices just until coarsely ground or desired consistency. Add the hazelnuts, salt, and pepper, crushing nuts slightly. Remove carrots from the oven. Drizzle with 1 tablespoon honey; toss to evenly coat. Sprinkle carrots with half the hazelnut mixture. Roast for 5 to 10 minutes more or until carrots are tender.
5. To serve, transfer carrots to a serving platter. Sprinkle with a little more of the hazelnut mixture. If desired, drizzle with additional honey. Makes 6 servings.

Food

Gingerbread Cake Roll

This elegant cake roll takes humble gingerbread to new heights.

WHAT YOU NEED

1 recipe Almond Pastry Cream
4 eggs
½ cup all-purpose flour
1 teaspoon baking powder
1 teaspoon ground ginger
¾ teaspoon ground cinnamon
½ teaspoon salt
¼ teaspoon ground cloves
⅓ cup molasses
½ cup granulated sugar
 Powdered sugar
1 recipe Maple Glaze
¼ cup sliced almonds, toasted

WHAT YOU DO

1. Prepare Almond Pastry Cream; chill as directed. Separate eggs. Allow egg whites and yolks to stand at room temperature for 30 minutes. Meanwhile, grease a 15×10×1-inch baking pan. Line bottom of pan with waxed paper or parchment paper; grease paper. Set pan aside. In a medium bowl stir together flour, baking powder, ginger, cinnamon, salt, and cloves; set aside.
2. Preheat oven to 375°F. In a medium mixing bowl beat egg yolks with an electric mixer on high speed about 5 minutes or until thick and lemon color. Beat in molasses just until combined.
3. Thoroughly wash beaters. In a large mixing bowl beat egg whites on medium speed until soft peaks form (tips curl). Gradually add granulated sugar, beating until stiff peaks form (tips stand straight). Fold egg yolk mixture into beaten egg whites. Sprinkle flour mixture over egg mixture; fold in gently just until combined. Spread batter evenly in the prepared baking pan.
4. Bake for 12 to 15 minutes or until cake springs back when lightly touched. Immediately loosen edges of cake from pan and turn cake out onto a clean kitchen towel sprinkled with powdered sugar. Remove waxed paper from cake. Roll towel and cake into a spiral, starting from a short side. Cool on a wire rack. Meanwhile, prepare Maple Glaze.
5. Unroll cake; remove towel. Spread cake with Almond Pastry Cream to within 1 inch of the edges. Roll up cake; trim ends. Drizzle with Maple Glaze and sprinkle with almonds. Cover and chill up to 6 hours. Makes 10 servings.

GINGERBREAD CAKE ROLL

Almond Pastry Cream: In a medium-size heavy saucepan combine ½ cup granulated sugar, 4 teaspoons cornstarch, and ¼ teaspoon salt. Gradually stir in 2 cups half-and-half or light cream. Cook and stir over medium heat until thickened and bubbly. Cook and stir for 1 minute more. Gradually stir half the cream mixture into 4 lightly beaten egg yolks. Return yolk mixture to the pan. Bring to boiling; reduce heat. Cook and stir for 2 minutes. Remove from heat. Strain into a bowl. Stir in ½ teaspoon almond extract. Place bowl with the pastry cream in a larger bowl of ice water; let stand for 5 minutes, stirring occasionally. Cover surface with plastic wrap. Chill for 4 hours or until cold; do not stir.

Maple Glaze: In a small bowl combine 1¼ cups powdered sugar and 2 tablespoons pure maple syrup. Stir in 1 to 2 teaspoons milk, 1 teaspoon at a time, to make a drizzling consistency.

Gianduja Mousse Cake

Gianduja (zhahn-DOO-yah) is a hazelnut-flavor chocolate from Switzerland.

WHAT YOU NEED

½ cup finely crushed vanilla wafers
½ cup finely chopped hazelnuts
2 tablespoons butter, melted
1 recipe Hazelnut Butter
8 ounces bittersweet or semisweet chocolate, chopped
8 ounces milk chocolate, chopped
1 cup purchased chocolate-hazelnut spread
6 eggs
½ cup sugar
1 cup whipping cream
 Whipped cream (optional)
 Unsweetened cocoa powder (optional)
 Coarsely chopped toasted hazelnuts (optional)

WHAT YOU DO

1. Preheat oven to 350°F. Butter the bottom and sides of a 10-inch springform pan. Wrap outside of pan tightly with heavy foil; set aside. For crust, in a small bowl stir together crushed vanilla wafers and the ½ cup chopped hazelnuts. Drizzle with melted butter; toss gently to coat. Press crust mixture evenly onto the bottom of the prepared springform pan.
2. Prepare Hazelnut Butter; set aside. In a large saucepan stir bittersweet chocolate and milk chocolate over low heat until melted and smooth. Remove from heat. Stir in Hazelnut Butter and chocolate-hazelnut spread.
3. In an extra-large mixing bowl beat eggs with an electric mixer on medium speed until frothy. Gradually add sugar, beating on medium-high speed until mixture is thick, pale, and holds a slowly dissolved ribbon when beaters are lifted. (This will take about 5 minutes in a heavy-duty mixer and about 9 minutes with a handheld mixer.) Pour chocolate mixture into egg mixture, stirring gently to combine.
4. In a medium mixing bowl beat whipping cream on medium speed until soft peaks form (tips curl). Gently fold whipped cream into chocolate mixture. Pour chocolate mixture onto crust, spreading evenly.
5. Place springform pan in a shallow roasting pan. Place roasting pan on oven rack. Pour enough hot water into the roasting pan to reach halfway up sides of springform pan. Bake for 1¼ hours. Turn off oven; let cake stand in oven with door closed for 45 minutes.
6. Carefully remove springform pan from water. Cool cake in pan on a wire rack for 2 hours. Loosen cake from sides of pan. Remove foil from pan. Cover and chill for 4 to 24 hours.
7. Let stand at room temperature for 30 minutes before serving. Remove sides of springform pan. If desired, top cake with whipped cream and sprinkle with cocoa powder and additional hazelnuts. Makes 16 servings.
Hazelnut Butter: Place 1 cup toasted hazelnuts in a food processor. Cover and process until a paste forms. Add 2 tablespoons vegetable oil. Cover and process with on/off pulses until combined.

GIANDUJA MOUSSE CAKE

Make-Ahead Sides

Guests may come to the table for the main event, but they stay for the sides. Get a jump-start on dinner with these prep-ahead dishes.

PILLOW ROLLS
recipe on page 108

OYSTERS ROCKEFELLER
SOURDOUGH DRESSING
recipe on page 108

Oysters Rockefeller Sourdough Dressing

Pernod is a French anise-flavored liqueur. You can substitute vermouth or chicken broth, if you like. (Shown on page 107.)

WHAT YOU NEED

2   10-ounce packages frozen chopped spinach, thawed and well drained
4   slices thick-sliced bacon, cut into ¼-inch pieces
1   cup finely chopped shallots (8 medium)
3   cloves garlic, minced
¼   cup Pernod
2   teaspoons dried chervil, crushed
10 cups dry sourdough bread cubes*
2   cups shucked oysters (about 28 large), drained and coarsely chopped (1 pint)
½   teaspoon kosher salt
½   teaspoon ground black pepper
1   14.5-ounce can chicken broth
2   tablespoons butter, melted
¼   teaspoon bottled hot pepper sauce
½   cup finely shredded Parmesan cheese (2 ounces)
    Bottled hot pepper sauce (optional)

WHAT YOU DO

1. Grease a 3-quart rectangular baking dish; set aside. Squeeze excess liquid from spinach; set aside.
2. In a large skillet cook bacon over medium heat until crisp. Using a slotted spoon, remove bacon and drain on paper towels, reserving 2 tablespoons drippings in skillet. Add shallots and garlic to the reserved drippings. Cook for 4 to 5 minutes or until shallots are tender. Carefully add Pernod, stirring to scrape up any crusty browned bits from bottom of skillet. Stir in spinach and chervil.
3. In a large bowl combine bacon, spinach mixture, bread cubes, oysters, salt, and black pepper. In a small bowl combine broth, melted butter, and ¼ teaspoon hot pepper sauce. Drizzle broth mixture over bread mixture, tossing to moisten. Transfer to the prepared baking dish. Cover with foil and chill up to 24 hours.**
4. Preheat oven to 350°F. Bake, covered, for 40 minutes. Sprinkle with cheese. Bake, uncovered, about 15 minutes more or until heated through. If desired, serve with additional hot pepper sauce. Makes 10 servings.

*Tip: To dry bread cubes, spread bread cubes in a single layer in a shallow pan. Let stand overnight on the counter. (Or bake in a 300°F oven for 10 to 15 minutes or until dry, stirring once or twice.)
**Tip: To serve right away, do not chill stuffing. Preheat oven to 350°F. Bake, covered, for 30 minutes. Sprinkle with cheese. Bake, uncovered, about 15 minutes more or until heated through. Serve as directed.

Pillow Rolls

These potato-infused rolls get their name from their soft and fluffy texture. (Shown on page 106.)

WHAT YOU NEED

4¼ to 4¾ cups all-purpose flour
1   package active dry yeast
1½ cups warm water (120°F to 130°F)
½   cup mashed cooked potato*
⅓   cup butter, melted
¼   cup sugar
1¼ teaspoons salt
2   tablespoons butter, melted

WHAT YOU DO

1. In a large bowl combine 2 cups of the flour and the yeast. Add the warm water, mashed potato, ⅓ cup melted butter, sugar, and salt. Beat with an electric mixer on medium speed for 30 seconds, scraping sides of bowl constantly. Beat on high speed for 3 minutes. Using a wooden spoon, stir in as much of the remaining flour as you can.
2. Turn dough out onto a lightly floured surface. Knead in enough of the remaining flour to make a moderately soft dough that is smooth and elastic (3 to 5 minutes total). Shape dough into a ball. Place in a lightly greased bowl, turning once to grease surface of dough. Cover and chill for 2 to 24 hours.
3. Punch dough down. Turn dough out onto a lightly floured surface. Cover and let rest for 10 minutes. Meanwhile, grease a 13×9×2-inch baking pan; set aside.
4. Using lightly floured hands, divide dough into 15 pieces. Shape pieces into balls. Arrange in prepared baking pan. Cover and let rise in a warm place until nearly double in size (about 40 minutes).
5. Preheat oven to 400°F. Bake for 20 to 25 minutes or until golden. Brush tops with 2 tablespoons melted butter. Immediately remove rolls from pan. Makes 15 rolls.

*Tip: For ½ cup mashed cooked potato, peel 1 small red-skin or russet potato (6 ounces); cut into quarters. In a covered small saucepan cook potato in enough boiling, lightly salted water to cover for 15 to 20 minutes or until very tender. Drain; cool slightly. Mash with a potato masher or an electric mixer. Or use ½ cup leftover mashed potatoes or refrigerated mashed potatoes.

Mashed Potatoes with Gouda and Crispy Pancetta

For additional flavor, substitute smoked Gouda for the plain cheese, if you like.

WHAT YOU NEED

1   pound red-skin potatoes, cut into 1½-inch pieces
1   pound russet potatoes, peeled and cut into 1½-inch pieces
1   cup ¼-inch cubes pancetta (about 5 ounces)
2   tablespoons thinly sliced green onion (1)
¾   cup half-and-half, light cream, or whipping cream
2   cups finely shredded Gouda cheese (8 ounces)
    Salt and ground black pepper
2   tablespoons sliced green onion tops

WHAT YOU DO

1. In a 4- to 5-quart Dutch oven cook potatoes, covered, in enough boiling lightly salted water to cover for 20 to 25 minutes or until tender; drain. Return potatoes to Dutch oven.
2. Meanwhile, in a medium skillet cook pancetta and 2 tablespoons green onion over medium-high heat about 8 minutes or until pancetta is crisp, stirring occasionally. Drain off fat.
3. Add half-and-half to cooked potatoes. Mash with a potato masher or an electric mixer on low speed until nearly smooth. Stir in 1½ cups of the cheese and the pancetta mixture. Season to taste with salt and pepper.
4. Transfer mashed potatoes to a greased 2-quart baking dish. Cover and chill up to 24 hours. Preheat oven to 350°F. Bake, covered with foil, for 40 to 45 minutes or until heated through. Sprinkle with the 2 tablespoons green onion tops and the remaining ½ cup cheese. Makes 8 servings.

MASHED POTATOES WITH GOUDA
AND CRISPY PANCETTA

POTATO-APPLE GRATIN

Potato-Apple Gratin

Tart apples such as Granny Smith are a natural fit in this savory dish. It's a perfect accompaniment to a holiday ham.

WHAT YOU NEED

8   medium Yukon gold or other yellow-flesh potatoes, sliced ⅛ inch thick (8 to 10 cups)
2   cups shredded or finely chopped Granny Smith apples (2 or 3 medium)
⅔   cup sliced green onions or thinly sliced leek
4   to 6 slices bacon, crisp-cooked and crumbled
½   teaspoon salt
½   teaspoon ground black pepper
3   cups shredded Gruyère, provolone, Swiss, or Jarslberg cheese (12 ounces)
1⅓ cups whipping cream
3   cloves garlic, minced
½   teaspoon freshly grated nutmeg or ⅛ teaspoon ground nutmeg (optional)
    Green onion slivers (optional)

WHAT YOU DO

1. In a large saucepan cook potatoes in lightly salted boiling water for 5 minutes. Drain potatoes; pat dry with paper towels. In a medium saucepan cook apples in lightly salted boiling water for 5 minutes. Drain apples; pat dry with paper towels.*
2. Grease a 3-quart rectangular baking dish. Layer half the potatoes, half the apples, half the sliced green onions, and half the bacon in the prepared dish. Sprinkle with half the salt and half the pepper. Sprinkle with half of the cheese. Repeat layers. In a medium bowl combine the whipping cream, garlic, and, if desired, nutmeg. Pour cream mixture over layers in baking dish. Cover with foil and chill up to 24 hours.
3. To serve, let gratin stand at room temperature for 30 minutes. Preheat oven to 350°F. Bake for 1½ hours. Uncover; bake for 15 minutes or until potatoes are tender when pierced with a fork and top is golden. Let stand for 10 minutes. If desired, sprinkle with green onion slivers. Makes 12 servings.

*Tip: To bake gratin right away, prepare as directed except do not precook potatoes and apples as directed in Step 1. Do not cover with foil and chill as directed in Step 2.

CAULIFLOWER GRATIN

Cauliflower Gratin

A topping of panko bread crumbs and chopped roasted almonds gives this gratin a touch of crispness and crunch.

WHAT YOU NEED

1   cup panko bread crumbs
¾   cup finely shredded white cheddar cheese (3 ounces)
2   tablespoons snipped flat-leaf parsley
2   teaspoons snipped fresh thyme
1½   teaspoons finely shredded orange peel
1   large head cauliflower, cut into small florets (about 6 cups)
2   tablespoons olive oil
2   tablespoons Dijon-style mustard
¼   to ½ teaspoon salt
2   tablespoons butter, melted
¼   cup chopped, roasted almonds

WHAT YOU DO

1. Combine panko, cheese, parsley, thyme, and orange peel. Cover tightly and chill up to 24 hours.
2. Bring a 4-quart pot of lightly salted water to boiling. Add cauliflower; reduce heat to medium and cook for 4 minutes or until tender but still firm. Drain well.
3. In a large bowl combine olive oil, mustard, and salt. Add cauliflower and stir gently to coat. Transfer to a 1½- to 2-quart baking dish. Cover with foil and chill up to 24 hours.
4. To bake, remove panko mixture and cauliflower mixture from refrigerator; let stand at room temperature for 45 minutes. Meanwhile, preheat oven to 425°F. Sprinkle cauliflower with panko. Drizzle with melted butter. Bake on top oven rack about 15 minutes or until heated through and lightly browned. Sprinkle with almonds. Makes 6 servings.

AMARETTI CHERRY
CHEESECAKE PIE
recipe on page 115

Holiday Pies

Whether creamy, custardy, or overflowing with fruit, these wedges
of wonderfulness are a special treat this time of year.

ABUNDANT LEAF
CRANBERRY-APPLE PIE
recipe on page 115

COCONUT CREAM
BANANA-TOPPED PIE

Amaretti Cherry Cheesecake Pie

(Shown on page 112.)

WHAT YOU NEED

Nonstick cooking spray
1¼ cups finely crushed amaretti or biscotti
¼ cup ground toasted almonds
⅓ cup butter, melted
2 8-ounce packages reduced-fat cream cheese (Neufchâtel), softened
1 cup sugar
½ teaspoon almond extract
¼ cup half-and-half, light cream, or whole milk
2 eggs, lightly beaten
4 cups frozen pitted tart red cherries
2 tablespoons cornstarch
¼ cup unsweetened cherry juice or 3 tablespoons unsweetened cherry juice plus 1 tablespoon amaretto
¼ cup sliced almonds, toasted

WHAT YOU DO

1. Preheat oven to 375°F. Lightly coat a 9-inch pie plate with cooking spray; set aside. For crust, in a medium bowl stir together crushed amaretti and ground almonds. Drizzle with the melted butter; toss gently to combine. Press crumb mixture evenly onto bottom and up sides of prepared pie plate.
2. For filling, in a large mixing bowl beat cream cheese with an electric mixer on medium speed for 30 seconds. Add ½ cup of the sugar and the almond extract. Beat until fluffy, scraping sides of bowl occasionally. Beat in half-and-half; stir in eggs just until combined. Pour filling into crust, spreading evenly. Cover edge of pie loosely with foil.
3. Bake for 30 to 35 minutes or just until center is set. Cool on a wire rack.
4. Meanwhile, for cherry topping, let frozen cherries stand at room temperature for 30 minutes (do not drain). In a medium saucepan stir together the remaining ½ cup sugar and the cornstarch. Stir in cherries and cherry juice. Cook and stir over medium heat until thickened and bubbly. Cook and stir for 2 minutes more; cool.
5. Spoon cherry topping on top of pie. Cover and chill for 4 to 24 hours. Before serving, sprinkle with sliced almonds. Makes 8 servings.

Abundant Leaf Apple-Cranberry Pie

(Shown on page 113.)

WHAT YOU NEED

1 recipe Pastry for a Double-Crust Pie (recipe below)
1 cup granulated sugar
3 tablespoons all-purpose flour
1 teaspoon apple pie spice or ground cinnamon
¼ teaspoon salt
¼ teaspoon ground ginger or 1 teaspoon finely chopped crystallized ginger
7 cups thinly sliced, peeled apples (7 medium)
1½ cups cranberries
Milk or light cream
Coarse sugar (optional)

WHAT YOU DO

1. Preheat oven to 375°F. Prepare Pastry for a Double-Crust Pie. On a lightly floured surface use your hands to slightly flatten one pastry ball. Roll pastry from center to edges to about 12 inches in diameter. Wrap pastry around the rolling pin. Unroll pastry into a 9-inch pie plate. Ease pastry into pie plate without stretching it.
2. In a large bowl stir together granulated sugar, flour, apple pie spice, salt, and ginger. Add apples and cranberries; toss gently to coat. Transfer apple mixture to pastry-lined pie plate. Trim pastry to ½ inch beyond edge of pie plate. Fold under extra pastry even with plate edge. If desired, crimp edge.
3. Roll remaining pastry ball to ⅛-inch thickness. Using a pizza cutter or a 1½-inch leaf-shape cookie cutter, cut out leaves. If desired, make vein imprints on leaves with the tip of a table knife. Arrange pastry leaves on top of pie. Carefully brush leaves with milk and, if desired, sprinkle with coarse sugar.
4. Cover edge of pie loosely with foil. Place pie on middle oven rack. Line a baking sheet with foil; place on bottom rack to catch any drips. Bake for 30 minutes. Remove foil from pie. Bake for 40 to 50 minutes more or until apples are tender and filling is bubbly. Cool on a wire rack. Makes 8 servings.

Pastry for a Double-Crust Pie: In a large bowl stir together 2½ cups all-purpose flour and 1 teaspoon salt. Using a pastry blender, cut in ½ cup shortening and ¼ cup butter, cut up, until pieces are pea size. Sprinkle 1 tablespoon ice water over part of the flour mixture; toss gently with a fork. Push moistened pastry to side of bowl. Repeat moistening flour mixture, using 1 tablespoon ice water at a time (½ to ⅔ cup total), until all of the flour mixture is moistened. Gather dough into a ball, kneading gently until it holds together.

Coconut Cream Banana-Topped Pie

WHAT YOU NEED

1 recipe Pastry for a Single-Crust Pie (recipe page 116)
¾ cup sugar
3 tablespoons cornstarch
2 cups half-and-half or light cream
½ cup cream of coconut
4 egg yolks, lightly beaten
1 tablespoon butter
1 teaspoon vanilla bean paste or vanilla
1 cup unsweetened flaked coconut
½ cup whipping cream
4 ounces cream cheese, softened
2 tablespoons cream of coconut
3 medium bananas
¼ cup cream of coconut
½ teaspoon vanilla
Raw chip coconut, toasted

WHAT YOU DO

1. Preheat oven to 450°F. Prepare Pastry for a Single-Crust Pie. On a lightly floured surface use your hands to slightly flatten pastry. Roll pastry from center to edges to about 12 inches in diameter. Wrap pastry around the rolling pin. Unroll into a 9-inch pie plate. Ease pastry into pie plate without stretching it. Trim pastry to ½ inch beyond edge of pie plate. Fold under extra pastry even with plate edge. Crimp edge as desired. Generously prick bottom and sides of pastry with a fork. Line pastry with a double thickness of foil. Bake for 8 minutes. Remove foil. Bake for 6 to 8 minutes more or until golden. Cool on a wire rack.
2. For filling, in a medium saucepan combine sugar and cornstarch. Gradually stir in half-and-half and the ½ cup cream of coconut. Cook and stir over medium-high heat until thickened and bubbly; reduce heat. Cook and stir for 2 minutes more. Remove from heat. Gradually stir about 1 cup of the hot mixture into egg yolks. Return egg yolk mixture to saucepan. Bring to a gentle boil, stirring

Food

constantly; reduce heat. Cook and stir for 2 minutes. Remove from heat. Stir in butter and vanilla paste until butter is melted. Stir in flaked coconut. Transfer filling to the prepared pastry shell. Cover surface with plastic wrap and chill 4 to 6 hours or until filling is set and thoroughly chilled.

3. In a small mixing bowl beat whipping cream with an electric mixer on medium to high speed until stiff peaks form (tips stand straight); set aside. In a medium mixing bowl beat cream cheese on medium speed until smooth. Gradually beat in 2 tablespoons cream of coconut. Fold in whipped cream. Spread cream cheese mixture over filling in pastry shell. If desired, cover and chill for up to 12 hours.

4. Before serving, slice bananas ¼ to ½ inch thick. Arrange banana slices on pie. For glaze, in a small bowl combine ¼ cup cream of coconut and ½ teaspoon vanilla. Spoon glaze over banana slices. Sprinkle with toasted coconut. Serve immediately. Makes 8 servings.

Pastry for a Single-Crust Pie: In a medium bowl stir together 1½ cups all-purpose flour and ½ teaspoon salt. Using a pastry blender, cut in ¼ cup shortening and ¼ cup butter, cut up, until pieces are pea size. Sprinkle 1 tablespoon ice water over part of the flour mixture; toss gently with a fork. Push moistened dough to side of bowl. Repeat with additional ice water, 1 tablespoon at a time (¼ to ⅓ cup total), until all of the flour mixture is moistened. Gather dough into a ball, kneading gently until it holds together.

Rustic Pear Tart with Saffron Pastry

WHAT YOU NEED
1   recipe Saffron Pasty (recipe, right)
4   medium Anjou or Bartlett pears, peeled, cored, and sliced (about 4 cups)
¾   cup dried cherries
1   tablespoon lemon juice
5   tablespoons sugar
1   tablespoon all-purpose flour
¼   teaspoon ground cardamom or cinnamon
   Dash salt
¼   cup pear nectar or apple juice
2   tablespoons finely chopped

EASY APPLE-CRANBERRY SLAB PIE

   crystallized ginger
   Milk
   Sugar
1   pint ginger, cinnamon, or vanilla ice cream (optional)

WHAT YOU DO
1. Line a baking sheet with parchment paper; set aside. On a lightly floured surface roll Saffron Pastry into a 13-inch circle. Transfer to prepared baking sheet; cover with plastic wrap and set aside.
2. Preheat oven to 375°F. For filling, in a bowl gently toss together pears, dried cherries, and lemon juice. Add 2 tablespoons of the sugar, the flour, cardamom, and salt; toss to combine.
3. For pear syrup, in a small saucepan combine pear nectar, the remaining 3 tablespoons sugar, and the crystallized ginger. Bring just to boiling over medium heat; reduce heat. Simmer, uncovered, for 5 minutes. Add to fruit mixture; gently toss to coat.
4. Spoon fruit filling onto dough circle, leaving a 2-inch border of dough around the edge. Fold dough edge up and over fruit filling, pleating as needed and leaving center uncovered. Spoon any liquid remaining in the bowl over filling. Brush dough edge with milk; sprinkle with additional sugar. Cover the fruit in center of tart with foil.
5. Bake for 45 to 60 minutes or until dough is golden and filling is bubbly. Cool on baking sheet on a wire rack. If desired, serve with ice cream. Makes 8 servings.
Saffron Pastry: In a small bowl pour 5 tablespoons boiling water over ¼ teaspoon saffron threads; let stand for 15 minutes. Add 4 ice cubes to chill the mixture; set aside. In a large bowl stir together the 2 cups all-purpose flour, ¼ cup sugar, and ¾ teaspoon salt. Using a pastry blender, cut in ½ cup cold butter, cut up, until mixture resembles coarse

cornmeal. In a small bowl combine 1 egg yolk and 3 tablespoons of the saffron-water mixture. Stir egg yolk mixture into flour mixture. Stir in enough of the remaining saffron-water mixture, 1 tablespoon at a time, just to moisten the flour mixture. Gather dough into a ball, kneading gently until it holds together; flatten into a disk. Wrap in plastic wrap. Chill for 30 minutes or up to 3 days.

Easy Apple-Cranberry Slab Pie

WHAT YOU NEED
2½   pounds cooking apples, peeled, cored, and thinly sliced (7 cups)
⅔   cup granulated sugar
⅔   cup dried cranberries
¼   cup all-purpose flour
½   teaspoon ground cinnamon
1   17.3-ounce package (2 sheets) frozen puff pastry, thawed
   Milk
   Coarse sugar
1   cup powdered sugar
½   teaspoon vanilla
   Dash salt
4   to 5 teaspoons milk

WHAT YOU DO
1. Preheat oven to 375°F. Lightly grease a 15×10×1-inch baking pan. For filling, in a large bowl stir together apples, granulated sugar, dried cranberries, flour, and cinnamon; set aside.
2. On a lightly floured surface unfold one sheet of pastry. Roll into a 15×10-inch rectangle. Transfer to the prepared baking pan. Spread filling over pastry to within 1 inch of the edge.
3. Unfold the remaining sheet of pastry; roll into a 16×11-inch rectangle. Place pastry on top of filling. Moisten edge of bottom pastry with milk. Fold bottom pastry over top pastry; gently press edges to seal. Cut slits in pastry. Brush top with milk and sprinkle with coarse sugar.
4. Bake for 50 to 55 minutes or until filling is bubbly and pastry is puffed and golden. If necessary to prevent overbrowning, cover pie loosely with foil for the last 10 to 15 minutes of baking.
5. For icing, in a small bowl stir together powdered sugar, vanilla, and salt. Stir in enough of the 4 to 5 teaspoons milk to reach drizzling consistency. Drizzle icing over warm pie. Cool completely on a wire rack. Makes 12 servings.

RUSTIC PEAR TART
WITH SAFFRON PASTRY

In-A-Twinkling
Candy Coated

Candy Box Caramels

In a small saucepan stir 12 ounces chopped chocolate- and/or vanilla-flavor candy coating over low heat until melted and smooth. One at a time, drop unwrapped caramels from a 14-ounce package into the melted candy coating, then use a fork to lift out caramel, drawing it across the rim of the pan to remove excess coating. Top dipped caramel with sprinkles (jimmies), nonpareils, or decorating sugar or drizzle with additional melted candy coating. Place on waxed paper-lined baking sheet. Let stand until coating is set. Makes 44 pieces.

Pistachio- Cranberry Chews

In a medium saucepan stir 6 ounces chopped white baking chocolate with cocoa butter and 5 ounces chopped vanilla-flavor candy coating over low heat until melted and smooth. In a large bowl combine 1 cup roasted, salted pistachio nuts and 1 cup dried cranberries. Pour candy coating over nuts and cranberries, stirring until coated. Drop by rounded teaspoons onto foil-lined baking sheet. Let stand until set. Makes about 25 pieces.

Chocolate-Coated Mint Cookies

In a small saucepan stir 6 ounces chopped chocolate-flavor candy coating and 6 ounces chopped bittersweet chocolate over low heat until melted. Remove from heat. One at a time, dip 30 chocolate sandwich cookies with green mint filling into chocolate mixture, allowing excess coating to drip back into pan. Place coated cookies on a waxed-paper-lined baking sheet. Top with green, red, and/or white sprinkles (jimmies) or nonpareils. Let stand until coating is set. Makes 30 cookies.

Candy Cane Bark

In a small saucepan stir 6 ounces chopped vanilla-flavor candy coating and 3 ounces chopped white baking chocolate with cocoa butter over low heat until melted and smooth. Pour onto foil-lined baking sheet and spread into a 10×8-inch rectangle. In a small clean saucepan stir 6 ounces chopped chocolate-flavor candy coating and 3 ounces chopped milk chocolate over low heat until melted and smooth. Pour chocolate mixture over white mixture on baking sheet. Use a thin spatula to swirl. Sprinkle with ¼ cup crushed peppermint candy canes. Chill until firm. Break into irregular pieces. Makes about 20 pieces.

gifts

SHOW SOME LOVE

BETTER TO GIVE

Tell family and friends how much you appreciate them with handmade gifts that are full of heart.

Cool Coasters

Different tastes deserve different styles and these
fun coasters offer awesome choices.

On the Block

Raid the scrap bins at the local home center for these handy coasters. Cut to desired size using a handsaw and a miter block to ensure straight cuts. Sand surfaces smooth. A coat of natural wood stain and sealer show off the grain. Stick cabinet bumpers to each corner on bottom.

Easy Peasy

Have a few bottles of acrylic paint with just a few drops left? Use that extra paint to dress up cork coasters. Freehand doodle, use a premade stencil, or make your own stencil from stencil acetate. Choose colors that match the recipient's decorating palette.

Mapped Memories

Decoupage maps of special places onto square tiles to make a one-of-a-kind set of coasters. Back the meaningful tiles with felt to prevent tabletop scratches.

Beautifully Beaded

Coasters made from felt circles add a burst of fun to any room. Freehand-cut shapes or use circular items such as plastic lids as a pattern. Make center circle large enough to accommodate glasses. Use embroidery floss to sew simple stitches to tack the pieces together, adding tiny seed beads for decoration.

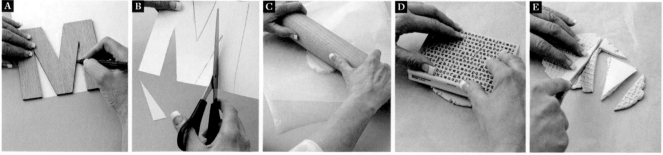

A Way with Clay

Intriguing textures emerge in these sophisticated wood and pressed-clay coasters.

WHAT YOU NEED

5-inch-tall flat wooden letter, ⅛- to ¼-inch thick (purchased or cut from plywood)
Pencil
Paper
Scissors
Oven-bake clay, such as Sculpey
Waxed paper
Rolling pin
Alphabet stamp or other desired stamp
Paring knife

WHAT YOU DO

1. Trace around the letter on paper, as shown in Photo A. Cut out as in Photo B, keeping the cutout pieces.
2. Place clay between sheets of waxed paper and roll to the thickness of the letter, as shown in Photo C.
3. Press an alphabet stamp or other desired stamp into the clay, as shown in Photo D.
4. One by one, place the cutout patterns on the clay; cut out with a knife, as shown in Photo E.
5. Place cutout clay pieces on a baking sheet, as shown in Photo F. Bake in oven according to clay instructions; let cool.
6. Using a paper towel, rub a thick coat of acrylic paint onto baked clay pieces, as shown in Photo G. Wipe most the paint off surface. Let paint dry.
7. Glue letter to wood backer as shown in Photo H. Glue painted clay pieces in place as, shown in Photo I; let glue dry.
8. Using a foam brush, coat coaster with clear sealer, as shown in Photo J; let dry. Apply a second coat and let dry.

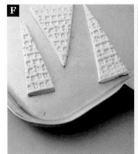
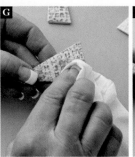

CHERRY-ALMOND DANISH
recipe on page 129

Rise & Shine Gifts

Give loved ones a delicious reason to get out of bed in the morning—
homemade muffins, pastry, jam, and hot cereal or pancake mix.

Simply Put

This bread is so pretty, it doesn't need much to make the presentation merry. Place the bread on a long narrow tray and wrap with a band of holiday-print parchment paper; tape to underside. Finish with a ribbon bow.

A Batch in a Bowl

A gift within a gift, this festive bowl is sure to bring smiles. Package pancake ingredients in separate bags; tie with ribbons. Nestle the bags in a mixing bowl lined with a holiday towel and tissue paper. Add in a colorful spatula and a bottle of your favorite pancake syrup.

CHOCOLATE-CHERRY PANCAKE MIX
recipe on page 129

CARAMEL APPLE JAM
recipe on page 130

Seasonal Scene

With all the miniatures available
in crafts stores, you'll have a ball finding
just the right ones to top your jar. Cover
the top of the lid with a circle of decorative
felt edged with metallic chenille stem.
Arrange miniatures and glue them in place.

HOMEMADE
ENGLISH
MUFFINS

Cherry-Almond Danish

(Shown on page 126.)

WHAT YOU NEED

¼ cup warm water (105°F to 115°F)
1 package active dry yeast
2 teaspoons sugar, divided
3½ cups all-purpose flour
½ cup sugar
½ teaspoon salt
½ cup fat-free milk
¼ cup butter, melted
2 eggs
1 teaspoon vanilla
1 12-ounce jar cherry preserves
½ cup sliced almonds, toasted
1 tablespoon water
1 recipe Almond Glaze

WHAT YOU DO

1. In a small bowl combine the ¼ cup warm water, the yeast, and ½ teaspoon of the sugar, stirring to dissolve yeast. Let stand 5 minutes or until bubbly.
2. In a large mixing bowl combine 1½ cups of the flour, the ½ cup sugar, and the salt. Gradually add the yeast mixture, the ½ cup milk, the melted butter, one of the eggs, and the vanilla; beat with an electric mixer on medium speed until combined. Beat for 2 minutes more, scraping sides of bowl constantly.
3. Using a wooden spoon, stir in as much remaining flour as you can with a spoon. Turn out dough onto a lightly floured surface. Knead in enough remaining flour to make a moderately soft dough that is smooth and elastic (about 3 to 5 minutes total). Shape dough into a ball.
4. Place dough in a large greased bowl, turning once to grease surface of dough. Cover; let rise in a warm place until nearly double in size (about 1½ hours).
5. Line an extra-large baking sheet with parchment paper. Place dough in center and sprinkle top lightly with flour. Using a lightly floured rolling pin, roll dough into a 15×10-inch rectangle. Spread cherry preserves lengthwise along center third of the dough, leaving 1-inch borders at top and bottom. Set aside 1 tablespoon of the almonds for topping; sprinkle remaining almonds on preserves.
6. Using a sharp knife, make diagonal cuts, 1 inch apart, along both long sides of the dough rectangle, cutting from each edge almost to preserves. Starting with a strip at the top of one side of the rectangle, fold strip over preserves; fold a strip from opposite side over preserves. Repeat alternating strips. Pinch ends under to seal.
7. In a small bowl beat together the remaining egg and the 1 tablespoon water; brush over dough. Sprinkle with the remaining 1½ teaspoons sugar. Let rise in a warm place until nearly double in size (about 30 minutes).
8. Meanwhile, preheat oven to 350°F. Bake about 25 minutes or until golden brown. Carefully transfer Danish to a wire rack; cool completely.
9. Drizzle Almond Glaze over top of cooled Danish. Sprinkle with the reserved 1 tablespoon almonds. Makes 16 servings.

Almond Glaze: Stir together ½ cup powdered sugar, 1 teaspoon milk, and ¼ teaspoon almond extract in a small bowl. Stir in 1 to 2 teaspoons additional milk, ½ teaspoon at a time, to make glaze drizzling consistency.

To Make Ahead: Prepare as directed through Step 8. Cover tightly with freezer wrap and freeze up to 1 month. Thaw overnight in the refrigerator. Preheat oven to 350°F. Bake about 10 minutes or just until warmed through. Continue as directed in Step 9.

Chocolate-Cherry Pancake Mix

WHAT YOU NEED

1⅔ cups all-purpose flour
⅓ cup unsweetened cocoa powder
¼ cup sugar
1 teaspoon baking soda
¼ teaspoon salt
½ cup miniature semisweet chocolate pieces, snipped dried cherries, or chopped toasted walnuts (optional)
¼ cup snipped dried cherries
1 recipe Cinnamon Cider Syrup or purchased pancake syrup (optional)

WHAT YOU DO

For pancake mix, in a large bowl stir together flour, cocoa powder, sugar, baking soda, and salt. Stir in chocolate pieces (if desired) and the ¼ cup dried cherries. Package mix in a plastic bag and tie with ribbon. Attach instructions for making pancakes. If desired, give pancake mix with Cinnamon Cider Syrup.

To Store: Transfer mix to an airtight container; cover. Store in the refrigerator for up to 2 weeks.

To make Chocolate-Cherry Pancakes: In a large bowl combine 1 lightly beaten egg, 2¼ cups buttermilk, 3 tablespoons vegetable oil, and 1 teaspoon vanilla. Add pancake mix. Stir just until moistened (batter should be slightly lumpy). For each pancake, pour about ¼ cup of the batter onto a hot, lightly greased griddle or heavy skillet. Cook over medium heat for 2 to 3 minutes on each side or until pancakes are golden brown. Turn over when surfaces are bubbly and edges are slightly dry. Serve warm. Makes 18 pancakes.

Cinnamon Cider Syrup: In a 5- to 6-quart Dutch oven bring 8 cups apple cider or apple juice to boiling. Boil gently, uncovered, about 1¾ hours or until reduced to 1½ cups, stirring occasionally. Remove from heat; cool to room temperature. In a small saucepan stir together ¼ cup packed brown sugar, 2 teaspoons cornstarch, and ½ teaspoon ground cinnamon. Add the reduced cider, 2 tablespoons butter, and ½ teaspoon vanilla. Cook and stir over medium heat until thickened and bubbly. Cook and stir 2 minutes more. Remove saucepan from heat; cool. Transfer cooled syrup to a clean screw-top jar. Cover and store in the refrigerator up to 3 months. Makes 18 servings.

Homemade English Muffins

True to authentic form, these English muffins are cooked on a griddle rather than baked. They are slightly chewy—with big beautiful air bubbles—and delightfully crisp when toasted. Slather with butter and marmalade and serve with hot tea.

WHAT YOU NEED

1 cup warm water (105°F to 115°F)
1 teaspoon sugar
1½ teaspoons active dry yeast
2 cups all-purpose flour
2 to 3 tablespoons butter, melted
1 teaspoon salt
   Nonstick cooking spray
6 tablespoons yellow cornmeal

WHAT YOU DO

1. In the bowl of a freestanding electric mixer* stir together the warm water and sugar. Stir in yeast; let stand about 5 minutes or until mixture is foamy. Add flour, 1 tablespoon of the melted butter, and the salt. Using the hook attachment, beat on medium speed for 5 minutes (dough will be smooth and elastic, but stringy). Using a rubber spatula, scrape down sides of bowl. Remove bowl from mixer. Coat a sheet of plastic wrap with cooking spray and place, coated side down, over dough. Let dough rise in a warm place until double in size (35 to 45 minutes).

2. Sprinkle a large baking sheet with 4 tablespoons of the cornmeal; set aside. Coat a 3-tablespoon ice cream scoop or a ¼-cup measuring cup with cooking spray. Using a rubber spatula, scrape down sides of bowl and fold dough over onto itself to deflate. Using the prepared scoop or measuring cup, drop dough in 3-tablespoon or scant ¼-cup portions 2 inches apart onto the prepared baking sheet. Sprinkle tops generously with the remaining 2 tablespoons cornmeal. Using floured fingers, gently push or pat edges of dough portions into rounded shapes (they don't need to be perfectly round). Cover with waxed paper and let rise in a warm place until puffy (about 20 minutes).

3. Lightly grease a large skillet or griddle with another 1 tablespoon of the melted butter; heat skillet over medium to medium-high heat. Coat a wide spatula with cooking spray. Using the prepared spatula, gently transfer half the dough portions to the skillet. (Try to get underneath the portions so you can pick them up without deflating them.) Cook for 6 to 8 minutes or until bottoms are golden, turning once halfway through cooking. Remove from skillet; cool on a wire rack. Repeat with the remaining dough, greasing skillet with remaining 1 tablespoon melted butter if necessary. Makes 9 muffins.

Tip: If you don't have a freestanding mixer, mix the dough by hand. Using a large bowl, combine the ingredients as directed in Step 1. Using a wooden spoon, stir the mixture at a steady rate for 5 minutes, scraping the bottom and sides of the bowl as you stir. Continue as directed.

To Store: Cool muffins completely. Place in a resealable plastic bag or an airtight container; seal or cover tightly. Store at room temperature up to 3 days or freeze up to 3 months. To serve, thaw muffins at room temperature if frozen. Split and serve warm with butter and jam.

Caramel Apple Jam

WHAT YOU NEED

4   pounds tart apples, such as Granny Smith, cored and chopped
1¼ cups water
2   tablespoons lemon juice
3   cups granulated sugar
1   cup packed brown sugar
1   tablespoon butter
1   tablespoon vanilla

WHAT YOU DO

1. In a large saucepan combine apples, ½ cup of the water, and the lemon juice. Bring mixture to boiling over medium-high heat, stirring constantly; reduce heat. Simmer, covered, for 25 to 30 minutes or until apples are very tender, stirring frequently. Press apples through a food mill or sieve to have 5 cups pulp; discard skins.

2. Meanwhile, for caramel, pour granulated sugar into a heavy 6- to 8-quart heavy pot, spreading evenly. Heat over medium-high heat until sugar begins to melt, shaking pot occasionally; do not stir. When the sugar starts to melt, reduce heat to medium-low and cook for 5 to 10 minutes or until all of the sugar is melted and golden, stirring as necessary with a wooden spoon. Remove from heat. Carefully add the remaining ¾ cup water (caramel will spatter and become hard). Return to heat; cook and stir over medium heat until caramel is dissolved.

3. Carefully add the 5 cups apple pulp and brown sugar to caramel (again, caramel will spatter and become hard). Cook over medium heat until brown sugar and caramel are dissolved, stirring constantly. Increase heat to medium-high. Boil gently, uncovered, about 10 minutes or until jam is thickened, stirring frequently. Remove from heat. Stir in butter and vanilla.

4. Ladle hot jam into hot sterilized half-pint canning jars, leaving ¼-inch headspace. Wipe jar rims; adjust lids and screw bands.

5. Process filled jars in a boiling-water canner for 10 minutes (start timing when water returns to boiling). Remove jars from canner; cool on wire racks. Makes 6 half-pints.

Fruit and Nuts Oatmeal

WHAT YOU NEED

2   cups regular rolled oats
½   cup coarsely chopped pecans, walnuts, or almonds
⅔   cup nonfat dry milk powder
¼   cup packed brown sugar
2   teaspoons ground cinnamon, apple pie spice, or pumpkin pie spice
½   teaspoon salt
⅓   cup toasted wheat germ
½   cup snipped dried fruit, such as apricots, peaches, pitted dates, figs, and/or apples or dried fruit, such as tart red cherries, raisins, golden raisins, blueberries, and/or cranberries
    Honey (optional)

WHAT YOU DO

1. Preheat oven to 350°F. Spread oats and nuts in a shallow baking pan. Bake for 15 to 20 minutes or until oats are lightly browned, stirring twice. Cool in pan on a wire rack.

2. In a 1-quart glass jar layer ingredients in this order: half the oat mixture, all the dry milk powder, brown sugar, cinnamon, salt, wheat germ, dried fruit, and the remaining oat mixture. Tap jar gently on the counter to settle each layer before adding the next. If desired, give a jar of honey with the oatmeal. Attach directions (below) for serving oatmeal.

For 2 servings: Before using, shake ingredients in jar to mix. In a medium saucepan bring 1½ cups water and, if desired, 1 tablespoon butter to boiling. Add ⅔ cup of the jar contents; reduce heat. Simmer, uncovered, for 10 to 12 minutes or until oatmeal reaches desired consistency (oatmeal will thicken slightly as it cools). Let stand for 1 to 2 minutes before serving. If desired, drizzle oatmeal with honey.

For 1 serving in a microwave: Before using, shake ingredients in jar to mix. In a large microwave-safe cereal bowl combine ¾ cup water, ⅓ cup of the jar contents and, if desired, 1 teaspoon butter. Microwave, uncovered, on 50 percent power (medium) for 8 to 10 minutes or until oatmeal reaches desired consistency (oatmeal will thicken slightly as it cools). Let stand for 1 minute before serving. If desired, drizzle oatmeal with honey.

Dolled Up

Yarn pom-poms made in holiday hues dress up a jar lid in a jiffy. Make one extra-special by tying a coordinating jingle in the center. Loop a length of ribbon, top with the pom-pom, and hot glue trim in place.

FRUIT AND NUTS OATMEAL

Warm & Cozy

Use basic crochet stitches to transform a few skeins of soft and snuggly yarn into the prettiest cold weather gear.

To Infinity

Try the basic technique used in making granny squares to crochet a versatile and warm infinity scarf. Use a collection of coordinating colors, depending on what your gift recipient will like, and consider whipping up an extra or two for last-minute presents.

WHAT YOU NEED

Worsted weight yarn: 1 skein cream and 1 skein each of four coordinating colors (such as teal, gray, brown, and aqua)

Size J crochet hook

Note: Gauge is not critical to the success of this project.

WHAT YOU DO

Foundation Rnd: With cream, ch 132, join with sl st to beg ch, being careful not to twist.

Rnd 1: Ch 2 (counts as first hdc), hdc in each ch around, join with sl st to beg ch 2 (132 hdc).

Rnd 2: Ch 3, 2 dc in same st (first dc cluster made). *Ch 1, sk 3 hdc, 3 dc in next hdc**. Rep from * to ** around. Ch 1, sl st in top of first dc, sl st in next 2 sts, and in ch-1 sp. Fasten off (33 dc clusters) (33 ch-1 spaces).

Rnd 3: Attach new color yarn in any ch-1 space. Ch 3, 2 dc in same space. *Ch 1, 3 dc in next ch-1 sp **. Rep from * to ** around last ch-1 sp, ch 1, sl st in top of first dc, sl st in next sts, and in ch-1 sp. End yarn. (33 dc clusters) (33 ch-1 spaces).

Rnds 4–12: Rep Row 3, changing colors each round. At end of Row 12, do not cut yarn. Continue to Row 13.

Rnd 13: Continuing with color used in Row 12, ch 2, hdc in each st and ch-1 sp around. Fasten off and weave in ends.

Cozy Toes

Keep toes warm in a pair of crocheted wool slippers. The two-tone Mary Jane-style make these an instant classic.

WHAT YOU NEED

Super bulky yarn: 1 skein blue (A) and 1 skein light gray (B)

Size K crochet hook or size needed to obtain gauge

Tapestry needle

Two ⅞-inch-diameter buttons

Gauge: 8 dc and 4 rows = 3 inches.
Take time to check your gauge.

Finished Size: Women's size medium (size 8/9)

WHAT YOU DO

CROCHET THE LEFT SLIPPER

With Color A, ch 3, sl st to 1st ch to make a ring.

Rnd 1: Ch 1, 9 hdc in ring. Join with sl st to beg hdc (9 hdc).

Rnd 2: Ch 1, hdc in same st as join and in next st. 2 hdc in next st. *Hdc in next 2 sts; 2 hdc in next st. Rep from *. Join with sl st to beg hdc (12 hdc).

Rnd 3: Ch 1, hdc in same st as join and in next 2 sts. 2 hdc in next st. *Hdc in next 3 sts; 2 hdc in next st. Rep from *. Join with sl st to beg hdc (15 hdc).

Rnd 4: Ch 1, hdc in same st as join and in next 3 sts. 2 hdc in next st. *Hdc in next 4 sts; 2 hdc in next st. Rep from *. Join with sl st to beg hdc (18 hdc).

Rnd 5: Ch 1, hdc in same st as join and in each st around. Join with sl st to beg hdc (18 hdc). Fasten off.

With Color B, join with sl st in 6th hdc before previous join. **Note:** By starting here, the join rows from previous five rows will be hidden.

Rnds 6 and 7: Rep Rnd 5.

Row 8: Ch 2 (does not count as a dc here or in remaining rows), dc in same st and in each st across (13 dc). Turn.

Row 9: Ch 2; dc in same st and in each st across. Do not turn. Ch 13.

Row 10 (make strap): Dc in 4th ch from hook (buttonhole made) and in each ch across (9 dc). Continue to dc in each st from previous row. You should have a total of 22 dc (not counting beginning ch). Turn.

Row 11: Ch 2; dc in same st and in each st across (13 dc). Turn.

Rows 12–15: (for size medium slipper shown: Rep Row 11. Or for longer or shorter slippers rep Row 11 until desired length. Do not fasten off.

CROCHET THE EDGING

Fold the last row in half with insides together, and join end of row to beginning of row with a sl st. Ch 1. With the outside of the slipper facing you, sc evenly around the slipper and strap. **Note:** For a slipper with 15 rows, you should end up with approximately 55–58 sc. Join with sl st to first sc. Fasten off.

FINISH THE SLIPPER

With tapestry needle and yarn, sew heel seam together. Attach button to slipper so it aligns with the buttonhole when strap is buttoned. Weave in all ends.

RIGHT SLIPPER VARIATION

Work pattern as for Left Slipper through Rnd 7. Before beginning Row 8, turn you your work. Continue in pattern. Strap should be located on the opposite side.

Top That

Craft fun toppers for gift bags and packages that add wow to your wraps.

Jingle Bells Rock

Wide ribbon provides the runway for three shining stars. Tie each large jingle bell with a narrow ribbon bow. Hot-glue the jingle bells to the wide ribbon.

Suave Snowman

This handsome gent is sure to garner attention under the tree. For the head, use half a clear plastic snap-together ornament; spray-paint the inside white and let dry. Hot-glue to white cardstock; trim edge with decorative-edge scissors. Draw on a face using permanent marking pens. To highlight eyes, use a toothpick and dot with white paint. Cut a felt hat in half; hot-glue a ribbon band and trims to hat. Hot-glue snowman to package, adding a ribbon bow with a small jingle bell center.

Bright & Merry

Dress up a plain gift sack with a cheery paper banner. Adhere glittery letters to a strip of white paper trimmed with decorative-edge scissors. Trim bottom edge at an angle. Attach paper strip to a piece of glitter paper and trim a narrow border. Trim top straight; attach to bag with gem brads.

So Ornamental

A fabric bow, tied to a gift bag handle, makes a presentation jollier. Choose ribbon with a fun wintry print and hot-glue a glittered plastic ball in the middle of the bow for glimmer.

Completely Pleated

Turn a paper strip into a stunning dimensional trim. Cut a 2×12-inch strip from cardstock; accordian-fold every ½ inch. Hot-glue short ends together. Brush outer edge with decoupage medium and sprinkle with glitter; shake off excess. Hot-glue jingle bells in the center.

Falling Flakes

Make a purchased gift bag even prettier with the addition of felt snowflakes dotted with jingle bell centers. Choose a bag with a solid or simple pattern like the polka dot bag shown. Use the bag color to inspire snowflake colors. Use hot glue to attach the trailing snowflakes to one side of the front of bag. Add a jingle bell to each center.

In-A-Twinkling
Clever Cards

Simply Ornamental

Cut a 2½-inch circle from holiday-theme paper. Adhere to solid paper using glue stick; trim a narrow border. Embellish pattern with gem stickers. Glue circle to a folded piece of cardstock. Stitch a baker's string hanger.

Take Flight

Stitching adds quaint detail to this dove. Use patterns on page 157 to cut shapes. Adhere pieces to solid paper; trim narrow borders. Poke spaces along edges. Use baker's string to sew pieces. Glue shapes to notecard. Add lazy daisy tail feathers.

From Our House to Yours

This mini scene is so sweet, your recipient may want to frame it to enjoy next year. To make the card, use patterns on page 158 to cut pieces from scrapbook papers. Use decorative-edge scissors to cut the underside of roof pieces. On front of a folded piece of cardstock adhere pieces in the following order: House, chimney, front door, roofs, ground, tree trunk, and tree. Add a fringed circle for wreath and a tiny hexagon for tree topper. Using a paintbrush, brush decoupage medium on tree, rooftops, and ground; sprinkle with snow-like glitter.

Gift with Gratitude

Cut out a 2¼-inch square from paper with small holiday patterns. Use glue stick to attach the square to solid paper; trim a narrow border. Trim around a small shape from remaining paper along with a tiny rectangle; write "thanks" on the rectangle. Using a needle threaded with embroidery floss, make one long vertical stitch through the center of the square; knot floss on back. Glue the square to the front of a folded piece of cardstock. Use adhesive gems to make a shimmering bow. Glue the tiny cutout near top of motif.

Getting the Boot

All your gal friends will love getting this stylish beauty! To make this card, trace the patterns on page 158; cut out from papers. Use glue stick to adhere the details to the boot. Glue the boot and heel pieces to the background piece then to the front of a notecard. Hot-glue four buttons to the left of the side seam.

Thank-You Tag

This pretty little card sends a big message. Use patterns on page 157 to cut a tag from holiday paper and a message flag from solid paper. Punch a hole in the angled end of tag; thread with cord and knot. Write "thank you" on flag; attach with two brads. Use double-sided tape to adhere tag to notecard.

kids

LET THEM SHINE
Unleash kids' creativity by arming them with all the materials and how-to needed to make super-cool holiday decorations.

Playing With Clay

Have fun pressing patterns into clay, cutting shapes, and baking them in the oven to harden and keep for many Santa visits to come.

Color-Block Frame

Capture smiles in a fun little photo frame. Roll and impress three colors of clay using the photo for inspiration. Use a plastic knife to cut pieces for frame as shown. Roll four yellow pea-size balls and four smaller from green; poke centers with a pencil. Roll a backing piece of clay ¼ inch smaller than desired frame size. Roll flat and cut a piece of clay 1×2 inches for the stand tab. Bake as directed. When cool, glue a small photo in center of backing piece. Glue frame pieces atop photo, adding flowers and leaves. Glue stand tab to back.

Terrific Tag

No bow needed with a tag this cute. Roll dark green clay flat between sheets of waxed paper. Use a cookie cutter to make a circle, cut off bottom quarter using a plastic knife. Impress with a clay stamp. Roll a coil and press to base for handle. Cut a candle; press to base. Add a yellow flame; impress. Roll three coils from light green clay; press to base. Roll a pea-size ball from red, impress, and place on candleholder. Bake as directed; cool. Glue to paper tag.

No-Melt Snowflake

Craft a seasonal sensation. Use a round cookie cutter to cut a circle from flattened green and white clays. Snip off 1-inch pieces from edge of white; press onto green circle. Use a plastic knife to press a snowflake design into white clay. Roll small balls of white, red, and light green to detail the edge. Clip off one end of a paperclip loop; press into top of snowflake. Bake trim as directed.

Ornament Notecard

This card deserves personal delivery. Roll green clay flat and cut a circle using a cookie cutter. Trim with bands of clay. Roll a coil and shape into a bow. Bake as directed. Glue bow to ornament and trim to decorate a notecard.

Three-Tier Trees

Make impressive tree ornaments by pressing clay stamps or household items into clay and cutting it into a triangular tree shape.

WHAT YOU NEED

Oven-bake clay, such as Sculpey, in three shades of green, plus yellow and red
Baking sheet
Waxed paper
Rolling pin
Stamp for clay
Metal ruler
Paper; pencil
Scissors
Paperclips
Marking pen lid
Plastic knife
Wire cutter

WHAT YOU DO

1. Use a baking sheet for work surface. Place one color of green clay between a folded piece of waxed paper; roll to about ¼-inch thickness as shown in Photo A.
2. Lift top layer of waxed paper and press with clay stamp, as shown in Photo B; remove stamp. Repeat with two remaining colors of green clay.
3. Use a metal ruler to cut a strip from each piece of pressed clay, each about 3 inches wide and 1½ inches high as shown in Photo C. Place pieces together; press gently without disturbing designs.
4. Trace and cut the tree pattern, page 155. Place pattern on clay pieces as shown in Photo D. Trim excess using the ruler.
5. Roll and cut a ½×1-inch piece from red clay. Press desired stamp carefully into the clay. Press trunk to tree bottom.
6. Use the end of a paper clip to gently score clay seams to help pieces attach to one another, as shown in Photo E.
7. Roll yellow clay between waxed paper; lift top sheet. Cut out a small circle using the lid from a large marking pen, as shown in Photo F. Make a star shape in the circle using a plastic knife, as shown in Photo G. Roll a small amount of clay into a ball; flatten slightly with a stamp, as shown in Photo H. Gently press the small ball onto the star front.
8. Use a wire cutter to clip an end off a paper clip; press into top of clay star, as shown in Photo I. Press onto tree tip, as shown in Photo J.
9. Bake the clay ornament according to manufacturer's instructions. Let cool. If any pieces are loose, use strong glue (such as CA) to secure pieces together; let dry.

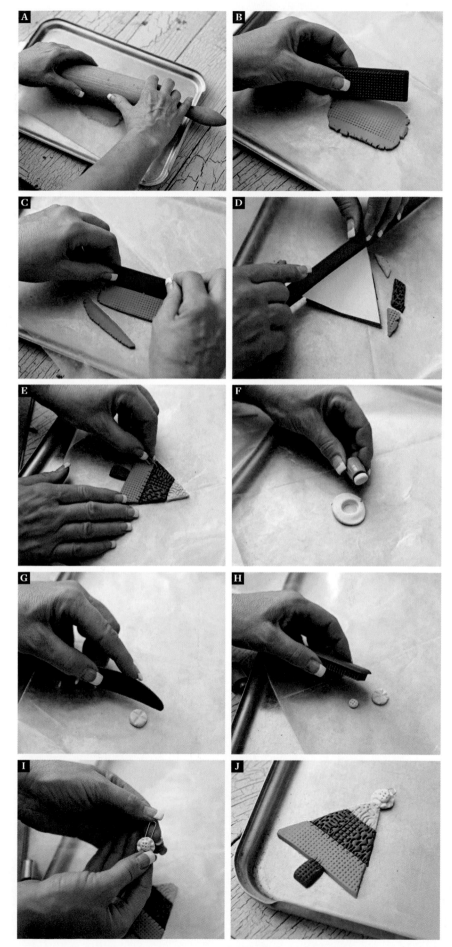

Snow Pals

Totally clever to look at, these snow folks are all crafted from socks and felt.

Bright Buddies

Welcome these cheerful, easy-to-make snowpeople into your home for the holidays! They're made with household materials, such as knee-high tube socks, decorative ankle socks, and rice for stuffing. Buttons and twine add cute accents.

WHAT YOU NEED
One midcalf or knee-high white tube sock
Rubber bands
Rice
Pair of decorative ankle socks
Twine or ribbon
Hot-glue gun and glue sticks
Assorted small buttons
Wooden skewer
Acrylic paint in orange

WHAT YOU DO
1. Cut off and discard foot portion of white tube sock. Turn the tube inside out and wrap a rubber band tightly around the bottom (where foot portion was attached). Turn the tube right side out so rubber band is inside the sock.
2. Fill sock with rice, pushing it down into sock as you fill. Fill sock until it stretches and is plump. Wrap a rubber band around the open end.
3. Cut off heel and toe from one decorative ankle sock. Cut off heel of other ankle sock. Pull the sock without the heel and toe over the snowman; center it on snowman for a sweater. Squeeze the snowman body at the lower edge of sweater, pushing the rice down to create a solid base. Tie a piece of twine or ribbon around the bottom of the sweater. Repeat, squeezing snowman and tying with twine at the top of the sweater, if desired.
4. Place the sock without the heel on top of snowman for a hat. Tie a twine bow around the toe end of sock. Hot-glue a button or other embellishment to the hat if desired. Hot-glue small buttons on head for eyes and, if desired, on sweater.
5. Cut off the pointed end of a wooden skewer and paint it orange; let dry. Hot-glue point to the face for a nose.

Simple and Sweet

Deck the halls (or your Christmas tree) with this pint-size Frosty the Snowman. He's made of felt, ribbon, and some polyester fiberfill stuffing for a jolly low-cost gift.

WHAT YOU NEED
9×12-inch pieces of felt: one each of black, white, orange, and brown
Water-soluble marking pen
Sewing needle and matching colors of thread
5-inch length of white ribbon
Polyester fiberfill

WHAT YOU DO
1. Draw a basic snowman pattern, arms, and nose onto white paper and cut out. Using a water-soluble marking pen, trace the pieces onto felt. Cut out pieces.

2. For each snowman, hand-stitch eyes, nose, and buttons to one body piece, using matching thread and running stitches and referring to the photo, above, for placement.
3. Layer the body pieces for each snowman with wrong sides together. Insert snowman arms between body pieces. Fold the ribbon length in half and insert the ends between the body pieces on top of the head for a hanging loop.
4. Using a scant ⅛-inch seam allowance, hand-stitch the body pieces together with running stitches and matching thread. Catch the arms and the hanging loop in seams as you stitch. Leave a 1½-inch opening in the bottom of each ornament. Firmly stuff each body with polyester fiberfill; stitch opening closed.

Snowflake Fun

Kids will be proud of their creations when they're displayed around the house this Christmas.

Forever Flake

Cast a wintry spell over the front door with a large wooden snowflake made from paint sticks. Tuck a few fresh evergreen branches behind the snowflake and secure them with florist's wire to introduce the sweet scent of pine. A pretty blue ribbon makes hanging this Christmas craft a breeze.

WHAT YOU NEED
Dinner plate
Marker
Newspaper (or crafts paper)
Large wooden crafts paint sticks
Crafts glue
Small and medium wooden crafts
    sticks
Wooden coffee stirrers
Bags of wooden crafts shapes in
    squares and triangles
White spray paint
Scissors
Ribbon
Hot-glue gun and hotmelt adhesive

WHAT TO DO
1. To make a template, use a dinner plate and a marker to trace a circle onto a large piece of newspaper or crafts paper. Divide the circle evenly into sixths.
2. Overlap two large paint sticks by ½ inch in the middle (for support) and glue the ends together to form the horizontal base of the snowflake. Repeat twice.
3. Lay the long sticks over the lines of the newspaper template, gluing at the center; let dry.
4. Repeat the same process using medium-size crafts sticks and glue to the center of the snowflake, so the medium sticks fall between the angles made by the large paint sticks.
5. Add two small crafts sticks to each medium stick at 30-degree angles and top with square wooden shapes.
6. Continue adding crafts sticks and wooden shapes to the snowflake, as shown. Glue in place.
7. When snowflake is dry, spray-paint it white. Let dry.
8. To hang, hot-glue a ribbon of your choice cut to the desired hanging length.

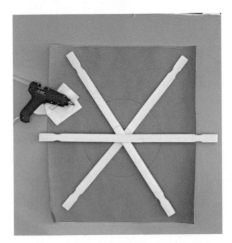

No-Melt Garland

Create smaller versions of the wreath to make interesting vertical garlands. For added texture, spray the snowflakes with fleck-style dimensional paint. When dry, hot-glue the snowflakes to wide ribbon, leaving approximately 2 inches between flakes.

Swedish Snowflake Ornaments

This contemporary take on classic Swedish straw ornaments combines crafts sticks and clothespins with wood rounds to create different snowflake forms. Use baker's twine to hang the charming snowflakes from the Christmas tree this holiday season.

WHAT YOU NEED
for the Clothespin Snowflake

Six small-size doll clothespins
Glue gun and hotmelt adhesive
Small- and medium-size wooden circles
½-inch-diameter button plug

WHAT YOU NEED
for the Crafts-Stick Snowflake

Eight crafts sticks
Glue gun and hotmelt adhesive
Small- and medium-size wooden circles
½-inch-diameter button plug

WHAT YOU DO
1. For the clothespin snowflake, glue the clothespins to the medium-size wooden circle, positioning them near the edge. Glue the small round shape to the center front of the snowflake, then glue the button plug in the center of the round.
2. For the crafts stick snowflake, overlap crafts sticks to form a snowflake shape and glue to the medium-size wooden circle. Glue the small-size wooden circle in the center of the snowflake and a button plug on top of that.

Paper Pretties

Add wintry charm to any dinner table with snowflake decorations made from paper napkins of any size. Cut chunky snowflake shapes from the napkin's folded corner. Unfold and scatter on the table.

Milk Mats

Here's a project that gets the whole family involved. Let kids cut paper snowflakes, then use them as patterns to cut the shapes from sheets of felt using scissors and crafts knife on a cutting mat. Glue them on contrasting thick felted wool for stunningly simple holiday accents.

Snowflake Silhouette

Give kids a handful of chenille stems and let them go to work making one-of-a-kind snowflakes that look stunning against Christmas tree green. Use cut pieces to detail some of the spokes.

In-a-Twinkling
Jolly Jars

Belted

As playful as Santa's elves, this jar is super jolly. Cut a 3-inch-wide piece of red felt long enough to wrap around a jar. Cut large zigzags along one edge. Hot-glue the felt to the top of jar. Use a narrow flea-market belt to trim jester-like band; hot-glue in place. Glue jingle bells to each felt point.

Hooked

Perfect for beginners, this mini scarf uses only a chain stitch. Have an adult show you how to do it or refer to the diagrams below. Make the scarf 10 inches longer than needed to wrap around desired jar. Crochet four rows. When done, make two 1-inch-diameter pom-poms and sew to scarf ends. Tie scarf around jar.

Antlered

Totally adorable, this Rudolph jar is perfect for sharing candy or hot-chocolate makings. To decorate the jar, cut four 3-inch brown chenille stems and wrap them around a longer piece. Tie on additional 1½-inch pieces to form Y-shape antlers, then hot-glue antlers onto the lid. Cut out eyes from white and black construction paper. Glue eyes and a red pom-pom nose onto the jar.

Repurposed

Trim square jars in a jiffy to fill with sweet treats for friends. Cut out pictures or designs from old Christmas cards to fit jar front. Use decoupage medium to attach the cutout to the jar. When dry, frame the card with chenille stem using a low-temp glue gun to secure it.

Initialized

A milk bottle is tall enough to hold an oversized candy cane upright. To trim it, tie a ribbon bow around the bottle neck. For personalization, use cord to tie a chipboard initial to the bow.

Patterns

SWEET RIDE
SLEIGH BACK
Page 36
Full-Size Pattern
Cut 1

SWEET RIDE
SLEIGH FRONT
Page 36
Full-Size Pattern
Cut 1

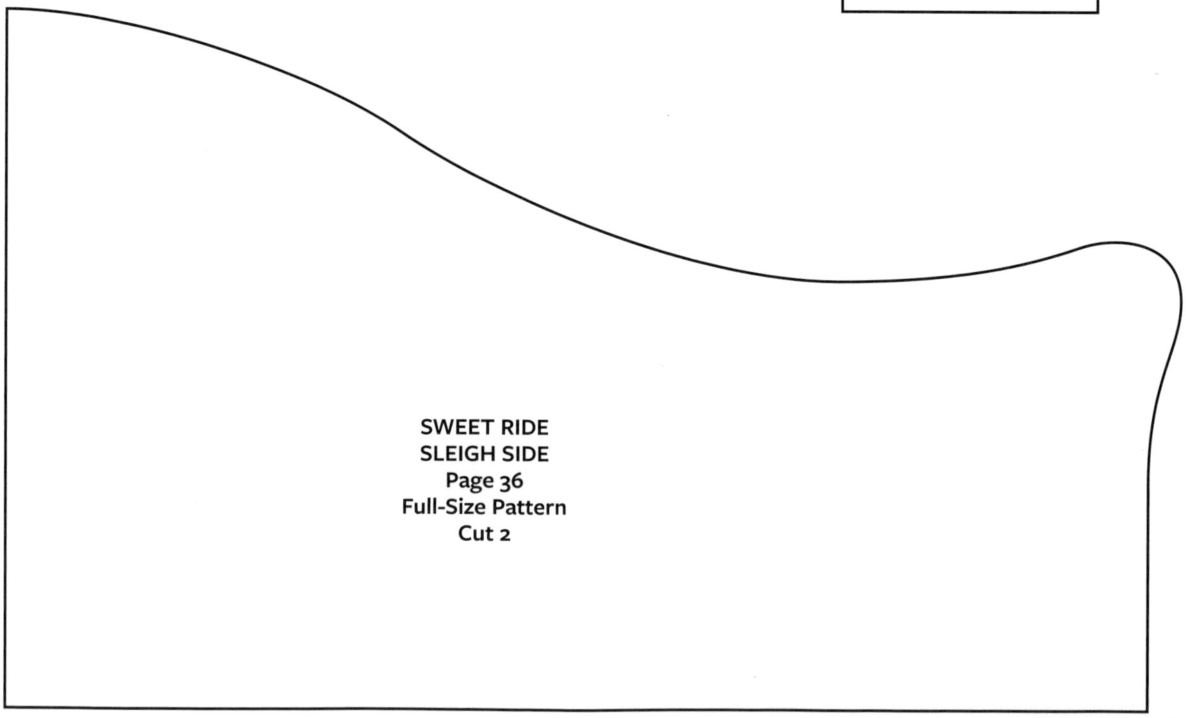

SWEET RIDE
SLEIGH SIDE
Page 36
Full-Size Pattern
Cut 2

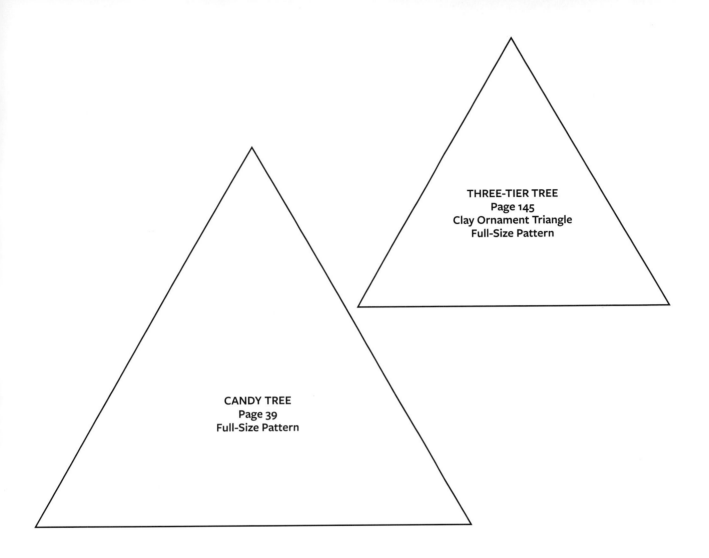

THREE-TIER TREE
Page 145
Clay Ornament Triangle
Full-Size Pattern

CANDY TREE
Page 39
Full-Size Pattern

SWEET RIDE
SLEIGH BOTTOM
Page 36
Full-Size Pattern
Cut 1

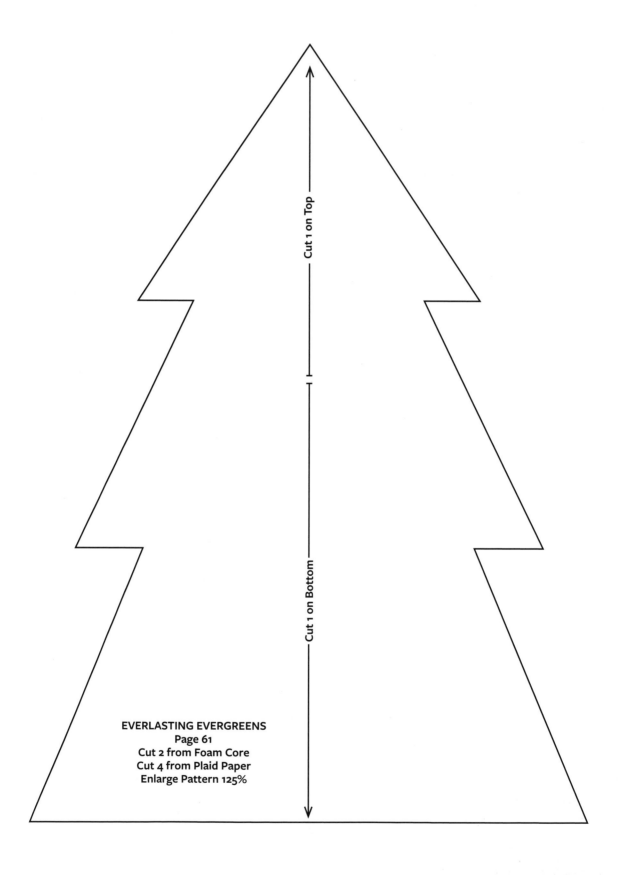

Cut 1 on Top

Cut 1 on Bottom

EVERLASTING EVERGREENS
Page 61
Cut 2 from Foam Core
Cut 4 from Plaid Paper
Enlarge Pattern 125%

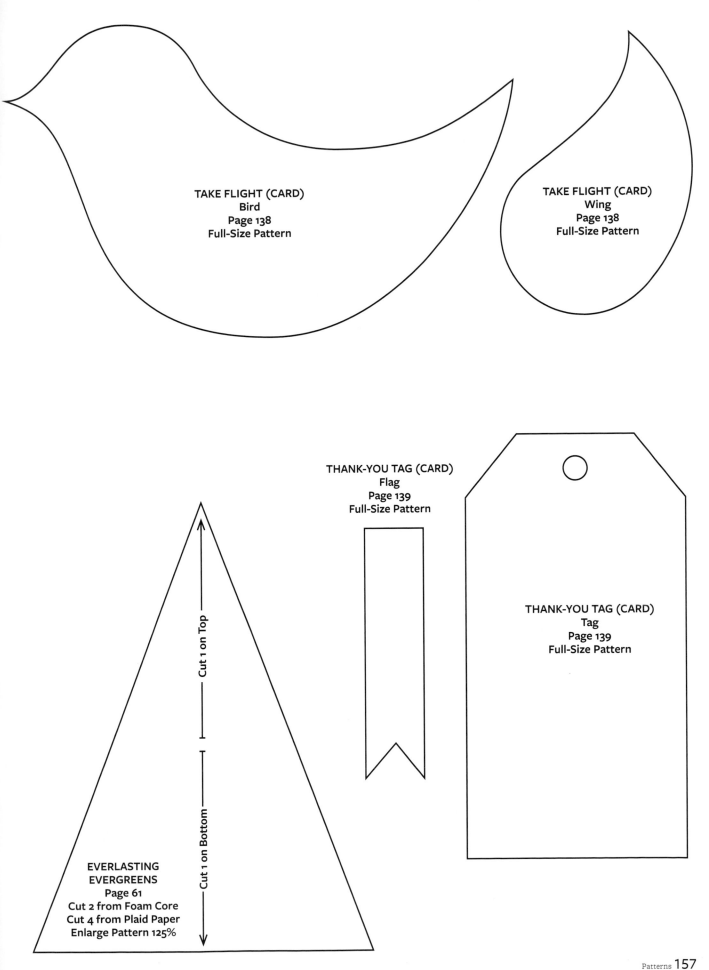

TAKE FLIGHT (CARD)
Bird
Page 138
Full-Size Pattern

TAKE FLIGHT (CARD)
Wing
Page 138
Full-Size Pattern

THANK-YOU TAG (CARD)
Flag
Page 139
Full-Size Pattern

THANK-YOU TAG (CARD)
Tag
Page 139
Full-Size Pattern

Cut 1 on Top

Cut 1 on Bottom

EVERLASTING
EVERGREENS
Page 61
Cut 2 from Foam Core
Cut 4 from Plaid Paper
Enlarge Pattern 125%

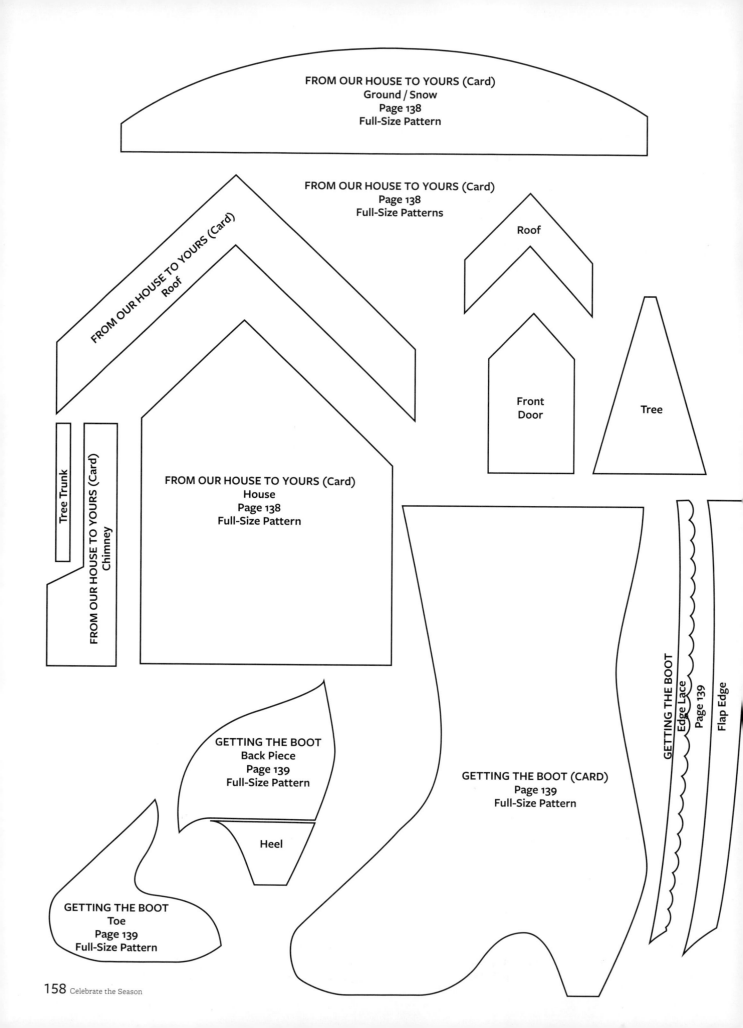

FROM OUR HOUSE TO YOURS (Card)
Ground / Snow
Page 138
Full-Size Pattern

FROM OUR HOUSE TO YOURS (Card)
Page 138
Full-Size Patterns

Roof

FROM OUR HOUSE TO YOURS (Card)
Roof

Front
Door

Tree

Tree Trunk

FROM OUR HOUSE TO YOURS (Card)
Chimney

FROM OUR HOUSE TO YOURS (Card)
House
Page 138
Full-Size Pattern

GETTING THE BOOT
Edge Lace
Page 139
Flap Edge

GETTING THE BOOT
Back Piece
Page 139
Full-Size Pattern

GETTING THE BOOT (CARD)
Page 139
Full-Size Pattern

Heel

GETTING THE BOOT
Toe
Page 139
Full-Size Pattern

Index

index *continued*